Software for the Self

W9-BFP-254

ANTHONY SMITH

Software for the Self

Technology and Culture

faber and faber

LONDON · BOSTON

First published in 1996
by Faber and Faber Limited
3 Queen Square London WC1N 3AU

Printed in England by Clays Ltd, St Ives plc

A CIP record for this book
is available from the British Library

ISBN 0–571–17768–9

2 4 6 8 10 9 7 5 3 1

CONTENTS

PREFACE

In George Gissing's *New Grub Street,* written a century ago, the character Jasper Milvain speaks as a representative of a new kind of artist – facile, clever, unscrupulous – who Gissing thought would abound in the twentieth century. Milvain sets out his creed:

> Your successful man of letters is your skilful tradesman. He thinks first and foremost of the markets; when one kind of goods begins to go off slackly, he is ready with something new and appetizing ... a Grub Street of today is quite a different place: it is supplied with telegraphic communication, it knows what literary fare is in demand in every part of the world.[1]

The arrival of the industrial system at the doors of culture was indeed envisaged as an invasion, and as a closing-down of a world of previously free spirits. Jasper Milvain exists as a professionalized contrast to Reardon, 'the old type of unpractical Artist, ... [who] won't make concessions'. Sustaining this tension between the (ingrained) old values and the (imagined) new ones was the fear that mass culture was anti-culture, necessitating a form of constant apology. The new industrial/commercial system propelled the masses into the arena of culture, and their arrival could be expressed either as irretrievable loss or as democratic fulfilment. Umberto Eco sees that moment as one at which the new 'integrated intellectual' would hail the placing of culture within everybody's reach.[2] But at the end of the twentieth century the sense of shock has, finally, been shrugged off. Television and radio, cinema, a proliferated theatre and musical culture, newspapers, magazines, cable and satellite, and the spread – via camcorders, e-mail, desk-top publishing, video-recorders – into the home of the ways in which all of these are distributed, have created an indifference as to whether a product of culture has arrived packaged and merchandized or through one of the traditional means of spectatorship or acquisition. The twentieth century has allowed many changing meanings to grow around the idea of culture, and these are records of the evolving interactions between technology, mass audience and tradition.

At the mid-century, the preoccupation remained the seemingly growing rift between 'minority' and 'popular' culture. Because intellectuals had given the label 'bourgeois' to much of the intellectual and imaginative work around them, the labels 'proletarian' or 'working-class' or 'popular' were uncomfortably, and often merely hopefully, applied to art that seemed to be 'alternative', critical, oppositional. But it was clear by the end of the 1960s that neither this division, nor its 'minority/popular' predecessor, any longer fitted the culture of our own time or the tradition from which the binary division sprang. 'The history of the idea of culture,' writes Raymond Williams, 'is a record of our reactions, in thought and feeling, to the changed conditions of our common life.'[3] Williams's own conclusion to *Culture and Society* demonstrates the difficulty of simply holding on to any of the then-familiar terms; there were only 'ways of looking at people as masses'. The tradition was multi-levelled and divided: even if the working class were to become dominant, to bring its own new values to bear and make its own contributions, 'the process would be extremely complex, because of the complexity of the inheritance.'[4] It was the sheer fact of the realized continuity of the artefacts of culture that rendered the labels ultimately too Procrustean for safety – or for clarity. And yet we cannot wholly jettison the century's jibes and labels: cultural things often still seem to be 'bourgeois', 'working-class', 'mass entertainment' or 'traditional'. And the very artefacts of a culture slip between categories in different periods.

My intention in these lectures is to take up some of the forces that are at work in the world at the end of the century and which are causing us to re-examine the definitions of culture both as context and as product. It is perhaps a pardonable (or anyway inevitable) temptation in an Eliot Lecturer to add to the hundreds of available definitions of 'culture'. For T. S. Eliot's *Notes Towards the Definition of Culture* have acted as a starting-point for all the more recent gyrations of the term since the publication of its first edition.[5]

The accumulating usage acts almost as a record of the history of the changing expectations that civilization holds of itself. The process of defining 'culture' can, of course, never cease, and the word carries with it at all times the precious cargo of its past. The intention in these lectures is not to conduct a further project of comprehensive definition but, more modestly, to take up four of the things that seem to me to be happening to culture in our own time, things that are, or ought to be, present in our minds at the end of this troublesome and complicated century. My first talk is concerned with the 'arts', which we often treat as the central operation of culture; but this unified term now possesses institutional, not to say bureaucratic, resonances that are part of the greater echo of the arts within the self, and these affect our ability to share the artistic experience. My second talk is concerned with broadcasting, now the most pervasive of the means of culture, and a technology where the institutional dimension always seems paramount; indeed, the surrounding institutional structure was part of the broadcasting invention, and the current wave of changes in the medium of television and its adjuncts is bringing changes within the forms of, and therefore the possibilities of, the medium itself.

The third takes as topic the new mental paradigm of 'information' that has been fitted, untailored, over the whole body of culture; it is as elements of an information economy that we nowadays absorb the materials of culture, that we monitor, justify, seek out, compare the artefacts which now shape the self. Finally, I draw attention to the promise, the cult (rather than the culture), that currently accompanies a newly emerging wave of computer-related technologies. These devices are bringing a new dimension of exactitude to the mechanical image, as well as a new dimension of interactivity, and raise the question of whether we are passing through a shift in the workings of the sensorium, the collective capacity of a society to receive, process and absorb imaginative experience. These four talks are, as it were, four separate mowings of the same lawn – not a smooth greensward glimpsed behind box hedges, but an unkempt affair, eroded by careless moles, neglected by absconding gardeners, the kind of lawn that demonstrates defiant disobedience to all efforts to order its affairs. My four topics do not define the whole, but rather represent great protuberances that ought to be heeded in any attempt at that greater task. Their presence helps to explain why the task has become so difficult.

Many people have helped me. I am grateful to three friends for reading the text (in earlier forms) before delivery as the Eliot Lectures of 1994: Michael Ignatieff, Ian Christie and Shusha Guppy have all made valuable comments, but none should be held responsible for the opinions or (mis)judgements expressed.

My gratitude goes to Robert McCrum and Julian Loose of Faber and Faber, who were responsible for the arrangement of the Lectures, and to Christopher Cherry, Master of Eliot College at the University of Kent at Canterbury, who made my stay at his college a relaxing and enjoyable experience. I am most grateful to the Editor of *The Economist* for allowing me to publish the article which appears as postscript.

ONE

Arts and Governments

In 1967 W. H. Auden, in inaugurating this series of Eliot Lectures, told his audience that our recent ancestors had feared social and technological change because they thought these would abolish traditional belief and the wisdom that accompanied it. Auden thought that artists would be driven in this century to take up either a pseudo-scientific stance labelled 'naturalism' or to remain in a camp of subjectivist aesthetes, excluding themselves from the world. This is not how things turned out, but artists have none the less remained locked into the 'in the world/out of the world' dilemma. Auden thought that the only business of poets (and I think he took poets to embrace artists in general) is to make objects which, as he put it, 'will remain permanently on hand in the world': that is, to make things which exerted their political presence only through time, and would pass from generation to generation and, in his phrase, 'break bread with the dead'.[1] Seamus Heaney, a quarter of a century later, talked in these same lectures of the 'stored goodness' of art, its efficiency lying in an audience's ultimate recognition of its salience, inscribed, encrypted into a medium. In Heaney's account of the process, it is through the deployment of stored goodness that the poet plies what he calls 'the government of the tongue'.[2]

The artificers of cultural products have long been enmeshed in this intractable dilemma, wanting to grasp the world, remake it and reject it; and it is noteworthy that they so often resort to quasi-political metaphors when they try to explain what they and other artists do. It calls to mind the tension between Samuel Johnson's claim in *Rasselas*[3] that poets are the 'legislators of mankind' and Shelley's retort decades later[4] that they were but 'unacknowledged legislators'. They sense a force within themselves which they describe or analogize as power. Their account of themselves often contains overt attempts at justification whenever they are placed under pressure from the formal social world. And their preoccupations are really with forms of power that are demonstrable only over time, beyond walls and boundaries; indelible but invisible power, magical and otherwise inexplicable power, the redeeming power of people who, contentedly or not, are in some areas overlooked or ignored by professional power.

But we live at a time when the arts and their step-sibling entertainment – with its uneasy, disunited relationship with art – find themselves more than ever entangled in politics. The arts are now drawn daily into wrangles over subsidy, public disputes over architecture, planning and design, debates about educational curricula, conflicts over the regulation of the new electronic media, issues of modernization, conservation and preservation. This is the new force-field within which artists in Western societies exist today. Moreover, the artists of non-Western or traditional societies are also becoming party to this nexus of dependencies. International bureaucracies impose their needs and nature upon art as meticulously as national ones. The tentacles of government, and sometimes its grudged resources, reach the garret of the most legendarily struggling artist.

The business of making symbols is no longer peripheral to the mainstream economy. The information industries, conceived as the vast amalgam of all symbolic and communication activity with the material support for such activity, now function at the centre of the economy. 'Art never expresses anything but itself' was the first principle of Oscar Wilde's new aesthetics.[5] But the artist, whether self-labelled as Baudelairean or Wildean outsider, is under pressure to behave as a player within an economic world. Academies have turned into lobbies. The artefacts of Art are now intellectual property. The *poète maudit* cannot get started without professional promotion and packaging. The modern, fetishized market-place, paraded and cosmeticized as an instrument of autonomy, only raises further questions about the nature of autonomy itself, the forms and measures of autonomy possible in the kind of society we have evolved. The market of today is perhaps just another shaping and constraining institution, offering art its special range of bargains and conditions.

True, at every stage of political history the artist has been offered that age's special bargains and conditions: painting, music and poetry were the emotional foodstuff of nation states, and today in a global economy they have become the support materials of tourism, design, international marketing, with a subsidiary political role as providers of prestige and the underpinners of new nationalisms. Unacknowledged legislation is subject to constant amendment.

It is difficult, even in this world of multinational, multi-ethnic, multi-perspectival uncertainties, to release ourselves from the tentacular associations of the nation state. The nation, shiftingly defined, is still the starting-point of all culture and much art. Hannah Arendt once arrestingly pointed out that, until the present century, the nation state had acted for the poor and deprived as a substitute for the privately owned home. The social beliefs that have gone with the nation, its tidy finalities – its claim to sovereignty – were moral substitutes for the kind of

[5]

personal autonomy only achieved by having an unsequestrable home of one's own. The state which emerged from the nation has become a giant holding company for all powers and institutions. Each effort to widen the private realm has resulted in more lines of control running directly towards the hands of government. The state offers an implied or explicit choice between efficiency in supplying our wants and its inexorable paternalism.

Parliamentary supremacy once meant something diluting, pluralizing, representative, but it has come to imply a ruthless wielding of centralized authority, the total effect rendering vulnerable a whole traditional conception of civil society. There has been in recent decades a diversity of inroads into accepted autonomies of all kinds, in trade unions, journalism, universities, metropolitan regions, local councils, as well as the professions. In Britain, the government has set up a Department of something called the National Heritage, mediating and making coherent, streamlining, appraising, constraining. The forms of state paternalism that have flourished since the late 1940s have given way to the newly opened private market, but a new public realm has also arrived, no longer mapped by a series of dotted lines but rather by ever-thickening lines of supervision and accountability ending in government. The state of the late twentieth century seeks not to direct affairs so much as to interpose its asphyxiating machinery of justification and accountability between private actions and public policies.

That is why the real challenge to the arts, as well as to all the industries and agencies of culture, now lies in the claim of the state to act, in the words of its prophet Max Weber, as 'the sole source of law and legitimate force within its own territory, and the sole appropriate object of its citizens' allegiances'. The operations of a culture depend upon the presence of a complexity of autonomies, untidy and overlapping. A century ago, the neglected Cambridge political scientist and Anglican priest John Figgis suggested that the moral test of a society lay not in the rights of individuals, but in 'the freedom of smaller unions to live within the whole'.[6] The spectre of absolutism returns to haunt every form of polity, and we are mistaken in thinking that the only available agencies of politics are the state and the individual. For individuals exercise their civic identity through the communities and associations to which they belong. A society in which personal rights are felt to be concentrated in individuals is a society in which rights are peculiarly vulnerable to governmental interference and in which individuals feel unprotected. We ought therefore to look at cultural questions as a range of actions on the part of small institutions and micro-communities. These are at the same time units of expression and bulwarks against absolutism.

In looking at the conditions in which the arts function, we are looking into the heart of an under-acknowledged contemporary dilemma. All the governmental machinery that has come into being to help the development of the arts and to regulate the electronic media imposes its own nature and interposes its own perception of society's needs. So we ought to look for new paths of pluralism, as well as fresh guarantees of individual rights. We need new public spaces on which the governance of cultural institutions can be founded, from which to confront this new outcrop of governmental authority. For the machinery of a modern culture to flourish, separations of power are required as much as access to state patronage and state subsidy. The arts in all their modern forms need an implemented understanding of the proper limits of government as much as they do its benevolence.

First, we need to establish how society came to acquire the arts, that is, in their formulation as a unitary entity, and to see what moral price came to be paid for this institutional construction. Then, in taking up the business of broadcasting, now a primary carrier of all knowledge of culture, we can witness the erosion of that public space from which the electronic media have been governed during their first seventy years of existence. That leads us to look at the modern paradigm of 'information', which is exerting its reductionist influence upon all cultural experience and shaping it into forms susceptible to modern kinds of regulation. Finally, there is the response of the human sensibility to these changing conditions of culture, one which is preparing us for technological (and therefore institutional) changes yet to be fully envisaged – which are not yet, in Seamus Heaney's phrase, 'encrypted into media'. The progressive arrival of perspective, printed text, camera, moving image, brought their own shifts in the operations of the human sensorium, and it is these 'trained' senses that prepare our expectations of cultural experiences; they transmute the 'dead poets' whom Eliot regarded as constituting 'what it is we know' into contemporary culture.[7]

TWO

The Arts in an Age of Bureaucracy

A train of thought was set in motion by a piece of junk mail – that treasury of evidence of contemporary motives, fears and aspirations. It emanated from a well-established financial services company, and its opening paragraph listed the company's arts sponsorships, the choirs, orchestras and arts festivals to which it had been contributing. An account of the company's capital-enhancing services followed. It struck me that something must have changed in the world of commercial institutions if sponsorship of the arts has become a positive selling point – after all, some customers might feel the company was wasting, rather than multiplying, their clients' assets by investing in such irrelevances. Perhaps the arts, or some of them, are acquiring a new role in our society, as instruments of reassurance or even legitimation; perhaps they now possess an ability to confer approval and evaporate scepticism.

During the 1980s the status of respectable beggar somehow came to be conferred upon the arts and their institutions by government; they acquired a kind of moral right of universal access to corporate resources. Governments were pressing industry to adopt the role of private patrons. The President of the United States, Ronald Reagan, had set up a committee of distinguished individuals to scan the private sector and stimulate it to provide philanthropic support to arts and humanities. Mrs Thatcher took similar steps, pressing philanthropy to take art where government shunned to take it. But it is uncertain whether these moves were the result of advances in social and political wisdom, or the outcome of some kind of new Faustian bargain between art and politics.

Today, to 'sponsor' the 'arts' is simultaneously to lay claim to a certain moral capital, and to suggest that one's enterprise is complicit with the values of a powerful and aspirant class of 'consumers' of the arts.

The new status of the arts has placed them half-way between the personal and public realms, alongside schools, hospitals, universities, pensions; they are partly paid services, partly civil rights. The traditional poverty of artists has been transformed into a kind of asset, part of their qualification for the role. For the arts have become objects of official arrangements and *provision,* and thus, concomitantly, of official deprivation. They have been given, after a struggle, the status of deserving poor and with it an acknowledged role within the economy. But one has to look back in time beyond the horizon of our own controversies to discover the origins and implications.

The arts began to acquire their unitary institutional form during the Age of Enlightenment, and as they acquired it they became a kind of substitute – a source of solace, perhaps – for all that was lost in the parallel phenomenon of secularization. And in the course of the same process, they acquired the burden of additional social expectations: they became objects of the belief that they could improve the condition of societies, transplant new hearts into nations, restore something that had been inadvertently abandoned as traditional communities turned into societies of mutually unacquainted people.[1] The idea has taken an ever more powerful hold and the expectations held of the arts have continued expanding.

It is puzzling to us in the twentieth century that the ancient world seems not to have recognized a common denominator among the arts, a generalized and unifying notion of the aesthetic. The arts were mutually associated not in terms of the common pursuit of the beautiful, but rather in terms of their common imitation of nature. If you accepted that painting, sculpture, music, poetry, were all different ways of imitating nature, you had to admit also a further range of imitating forms, such as magic and the skill of mimicking people and animals. Imitation was a unifying idea, but not an exclusive one. Another concept that did bring a range of artistic practices into a unity was the myth and metaphor of the Muses. There were nine of them, the daughters of Zeus and Mnemosyne (who represented memory), but these did not include any representative of the visual arts: the Muses concerned themselves with dance and astronomy, and with literature in seven different forms (epic and sacred song, comedy, tragedy, lyrical and love poetry, history).

The ancient world had also devised a classification of knowledge into the liberal arts, liberal because they were suitable for free-born citizens, as opposed to the vulgar arts, which were more suitable for serfs and foreigners. The medieval monastic education system took over this schedule, and seven Liberal Arts emerged as recognized objects of study, as the proper raw material of education; these arts are the ones that linger in the modern university's rubric for the degrees of BA and MA, and were more concerned with techniques of communication and of measurement than with the practice either of imitating nature or serving the Muses. The first three, the Trivium, consisted of grammar, dialectic (or logic) and rhetoric, and the latter four, the Quadrivium, consisted of arithmetic, geometry, astronomy and music. Medieval education undertook a number of refinements, relabellings and reorganizations of this grouping, and recognized other divisions of knowledge, but did not create the distinctions between 'arts' and other forms of knowledge, such as science, that would suit the kinds of categories we use today. Ghiberti, for example, recommends ten liberal arts for the benefit of sculptors, by adding medicine, anatomy and perspective to the seven conventional subjects.[2]

The Latin term *scientia* in Renaissance Italy implied a more generalized theoretical knowledge than did the Latin term *ars*, the latter containing a strong sense of the physicality of the art or skill concerned. But the whole conception of knowledge was meanwhile shifting from retrospective to futuristic mode, from dependence upon ancient models to researched discovery. Renaissance knowledge, aided by the printing press, was becoming subject to the process of progressive augmentation;[3] the discoveries of an individual could replace the certainties offered by classic exemplar. Nowhere was this more apparent than in the practice of painting and sculpture. Leonardo's perspective drawings of the musculature of human cadavers widened the possibilities of art as much as of anatomy. Where painters had relied on the detailed prescriptions of ancient texts for the proportions of the human body, for the arithmetical relationships between foot-size and head, between torso and limbs, artists now resorted to dissection, aided by new discoveries in the mathematics of perspective and their own recording of their observations. The art of figural representation and the knowledge of human anatomy advanced simultaneously.[4] Michelangelo and Leonardo both had experience of dissection, and the proliferating variety of their groupings of human forms and human movement demonstrates their escape from the pattern-book as much as it does the confluence of science and art.[5] Alberti had pioneered this transformation of artistic practice in his treatise *On Painting* of 1436: 'When painting living creatures first sketch in the bones ... Then add the sinews and muscles and finally clothe the bones and muscles with flesh and skin ... As Nature clearly and openly reveals all these proportions, so the zealous painter will find great profit from investigating them in Nature for himself.'[6]

Moreover, the fine arts, as they came to be called, were neither rejected nor neglected as material of education, but were scattered among the topics forming the Trivium and the Quadrivium; poetry, for example, was fitted into grammar or rhetoric. But philosophy was adopted as a grand linking subject, while painting, architecture and sculpture were felt to be still the natural preoccupations of artisans. The word 'art' retained its equivalence with the Greek expression *techne*; it was a transferable ability rather than a part of fundamental knowledge. The Renaissance seems not to have accepted that the aesthetic sense, present in all people, transcends and unites a variety of physical skills, and causes them to reach out towards the emotions; but the notion of artistic genius certainly did flourish. The gift of poetry, for instance, began to be perceived as the emanation of a special psychic quality, a kind of divine madness.

The visual arts were clearly dependent upon skills which were taught within the Renaissance school curriculum. Painting, for example, as well as sculpture, required a considerable knowledge of perspective and geometry. Leonardo's writings are explicit in showing the linkage between painting and mathematics. Moreover, the social prestige of painting had clearly come to equal that of poetry and music. Gradually, painting, sculpture and architecture were weaned from the crafts of which they consisted. In his *Lives of the Artists*, Vasari talks of the *arti del disegno*, in which one can see a foreshadowing of the later idea of the *beaux arts*;[7] in Florence there existed an Accademia del Disegno, which functioned alongside the literary academies. All of these had an evident basis in learning, in science, in historical literature. So had medicine and law and other pursuits of the learned, which possessed numerous shared affinities through their nature as learned activities. But the collecting of ancient coins, the arts of fencing and horsemanship, were also acknowledged pursuits of the learned, and no generally agreed criteria existed for separating such activities from others that we think of today as arts. Given the vastness of the literature and the depth of the Renaissance preoccupation with the origins of all the decorative and other kinds of art, it is strange that no generalized sense of the aesthetic took root, at least to the extent of providing a linked definition of the arts. Paul Oscar Kristeller worked through the entire, and considerable, corpus of literature thrown up by Renaissance Italy in its fascinated pursuit of those issues, and sees no hint of the modern system of the fine arts, or the *beaux arts*, in any Italian text until the latter half of the eighteenth century.[8]

Kristeller looks instead to France for the roots of the unitary idea of the arts. The Académie Française was founded in 1635, and was charged with the cultivation of the language and literature of France. Many other academies followed in its wake after 1660, several devoted to the visual arts as well as others to medals, the circus, inscriptions. They are perhaps better described in our terms as trade associations. But no system of consolidation was ever proposed, and no separation, linguistic or otherwise, is made between those devoted to trades and sciences and those devoted to decorative or other arts. It was in literary controversy, in the *Querelle* between the Ancients and Moderns, that the cultural distinctions between arts and sciences were brought out; the latter were evidently being advanced by the research and discovery taking place in the late Renaissance era. A demarcation naturally evolved between those intellectual preoccupations that were susceptible to scientific progress and those which were the continuous concerns of human society.

When, well into the eighteenth century, an idea of Taste, as a transferable and universalizing sense of the beautiful, emerged, it was fused with a notion of the beauty of morality and, more generally, of the work of the spirit. 'The taste of Beauty perfects the Character of the Gentleman', claimed Lord Shaftesbury, and the values of civic humanism acted as a powerful engine to all fresh theorizing. The imitation of nature was, however, revived as the primary of all the activities entailed in the arts. The rediscovered ancient concept of imitation now began to act as cement for the construction of an edifice of the arts as a whole, a moral home for the whole family of artists. And Public Taste was linked symbiotically with Public Virtue. In the Preface to Diderot's *Encyclopédie* it is asserted that this idea – the idea that a commonality of the imitation of nature existed among the whole family of art-forms, despite the different skills deployed among them – was now spreading throughout Europe.[9]

Thus it was that gradually, in a world that was adopting the gathered notion of *liberal* arts, separated from the physical and mechanical, those liberal arts began to lose their defining role as the activities merely of the noble. Diderot accepted that there was a group of activities which were 'fine' or, rather, *beaux*. Diderot's work bears the subtitle *Dictionnaire Raisonné des Sciences, des Arts et des Métiers*. The elaborate prefatory material to his *Encyclopédie* indicates how profoundly preoccupied people were at that moment with the business of categorizing the new knowledge.

Diderot informs his readers that the distinction between liberal and mechanical arts has had a number of bad and misleading effects. His own grand division is tripartite, into History, Philosophy and Poetry. History is based upon the faculty of Memory; Philosophy is based upon Reason, and is subdivided into the sciences of God, Man and Nature; Poetry is based upon the faculty of Imagination, and is divided into sacred and profane and thence into all the various familiar forms of literature. Under the same heading of Imagination he places music, painting, sculpture, Civil Architecture and Engraving. But this very thorough recategorization of human knowledge is qualified in his Preface.

Here, the principle of imitation is reasserted as the starting-point. Those liberal arts that are concerned to imitate nature may be called *Beaux Arts* because they share pleasure as their principal objective. Painting and Sculpture are chief of the forms of knowledge that depend upon imitation because they get closest to the objects represented and speak most directly to the senses. Next come Architecture, Poetry and Music. Music (as performance rather than theory) is the least advanced, because the musical models of the ancients do not survive into modern times in a form that may be imitated. Progress since the Renaissance has thus been comparatively laggard in music.

The term *Beaux Arts* went on to become the regularly employed unifying term, and this was confirmed after the Revolution when several of the older academies surviving from the seventeenth century were merged into a single *Académie des Beaux Arts*. But there was still no distinction made between the beauty of the physical objects of art and the beauty of the moral virtues to which they were firmly linked. The *Beaux Arts* were not a social institution so much as a moral force. It was felt that the *taste* for poetry, the ability to appreciate it, was a product of the moral sense rather than of a separate aesthetic faculty within the sensorium.

The belief in the existence of an aesthetic sense, of the talent of the trained spectator existing alongside that of the artist, is crucial to the twentieth century's establishment of the arts as an industry, or as an analogue of industry. Our predisposition to act as spectators, or rather consumers, of art is located in a sense parallel to that of hunger and thirst. If we were not prone to hunger, there would be no basis for a stable food industry. The evolution of the idea of the arts as fulfilling a universal human appetite has to be traced to evolving conceptions of the Imagination, which was, as it were, the holding sense, the faculty through which the sense of pleasure was transferred from one art to another.

Joseph Addison in 1712 penned a group of *Spectator* essays in which he 'considers the works of nature and art, as they are qualified to entertain the Imagination', and argues that there is something 'more bold and masterly in the rough careless strokes of nature' than can be achieved by the arts of the gardener or the painter of 'landskips'.[10] In working through his case, Addison refers to a range of art-forms, including literary description, statuary, gardening, architecture, painting. In his *The Pleasures of Imagination*, published in the 1740s, the poet Akenside takes up the same theme, praising the superiority of nature over art but drawing attention to a range of 'pleasing kinds' of art.[11] The arrival in London of Handel gave a great boost to new ways of thinking about the arts and the audience of art; his sudden and enormous social and commercial success gave a great fillip to the recognition of music as an organized *professional* institution. People realized that they felt a need for constant access to a repertoire of music. Lully had had a similar impact in France. The great public Commemoration of Handel in 1784 confirmed the presence of a new popular commitment to music, just as the Shakespeare Jubilee of 1769 had done for literature and theatre, and the founding of the Royal Academy in 1768 for painting. The flocking of audiences to open artistic events was without precedent; the recruiting of great urban crowds to come together to enjoy and to judge an artistic event was a new phenomenon. Historians began to turn to the arts as areas of special historio-graphic interest and expertise, and the wave of formal histories of different art-forms that arrived in the late eighteenth century helped to fix the relativities of esteem and give permanence to the new specialist publics, confirming their private and collective commitment to each form.

But it was in Germany that the new concept of aesthetics was turned into a subject for comparative study; after 1760 there were courses at German universities, with a host of tracts and textbooks becoming available as supports to a general theory of the fine arts. There existed a class of people who were artists; there existed an artistic public whom they addressed. Thus by the end of the eighteenth century the unitary conception of the arts was in a sense completed. Works of art could be studied and compared. The experience of these works could be held in the memory, and the resulting knowledge came to fuel a machinery of relationships between artists, middlemen, paying audiences, readerships, connoisseurs, amateur enthusiasts.

Within the institution of the arts, the artist acquired a special outlook, an apartness. Imagination is the special form of person-al power to which the artist lays claim and which sustains the group identity of artists. At times the artist has been self-repre-sented as rebel, as outsider, as criminal, but more frequently simply as a figure apart, offering his vision to an uncomprehend-ing world, rejecting the *quotidien* of society, bourgeois or other-wise. To many, the arts became a substitute for religion; for some, the two became fused in a shared psychic surge towards the sense of the sacred, the inward revelation. For many artists, art and politics became fused, the pursuit of art somehow enjoining a commitment to protest, to rejection.

The belief that the aesthetic condition of a society should

command the attention of government is associated in our minds with both Communist totalitarianism and with nationalism. At present, most people agree that governments should provide some sort of basic support to at least some arts. Most would probably also agree that governments should refrain from any deeper involvement, except perhaps to help draw certain formal lines of permissibility in respect of obscenity, violence, public incitement to breaches of the law. But when we look at the place of government in the arts today, there are several discourses bearing down upon us, including ideas that link the very existence of societies as nations with the flourishing of artistic activity. The rediscovery of ancient poetic traditions in Europe in the eighteenth century lies at the foundation of modern nationalisms.

Consider, for example, the outlook of Samuel Taylor Coleridge, whose ideas continue to nourish several different strands of the discussion. Coleridge started to think about art and nationhood in the decade that followed the lifting of the travel restrictions of the Napoleonic years. The world of Europe was open again, and its intellectual operations were again accessible. He lived in a country deeply influenced by Benthamite utilitarianism, with its vision of a world of individuals all in pursuit of individual interests and pleasures. Coleridge inserted a contrary conception, a *social* or organic way of stating the interests of a nation. England had passed through ideological conflict, draconian intellectual controls, an overseas war, and at home the industrial revolution had passed through its first phase. Coleridge often reminds his readers that the welfare of a nation (its *permanence* was the term he used) 'depends on a continuing and progressive civilization ... in the harmonious development of those qualities and faculties that characterize our humanity'.[12] That harmonious development he calls 'cultivation'. Whereas in the world of the eighteenth century cultivation had been a quality displayed by individuals, it had for Coleridge become a precondition for the proper functioning of a society.

Coleridge conceived an impossible project – one of his eccentric but instructive forays into the betterment of society – around the creation of what he called the Clerisy, which was to be a kind of official intellectual élite. These were to be funded by a foundation called the Nationalty and be based in an institution he called the National Church; this was not the Church as was known, for this would degenerate, he thought, into a mere sect, but would be an institution which would contain the learned of all denominations, 'the sages and professors of … all the so-called liberal arts and sciences'. The remit of this complex body, whose members were to be spread throughout the entire nation as resident guides, guardians and instructors, was 'to preserve the stores and to guard the treasures of past civilization, and thus to bind the present with the past'. He calls his Clerisy a third estate, after aristocrats and merchants. We might today call it an intelligentsia – a class dedicated to the extension and preservation of culture, or to repeat Coleridge's terms, 'the harmonious development of those qualities and faculties that characterize our humanity'.[13]

Coleridge was trying to look into the heart of a society in turmoil, and in one of his flashes of insight announced its need to be preoccupied not primarily with wealth but with art, or as we would put it, with the arts. He juxtaposed two forms of knowledge labelled 'substantial' and 'abstract'. The *substantial* depends upon a form of social organization, since it involves 'that intuition of things which arise when we possess ourselves as one with the whole', while the *abstract* arises when we 'think of ourselves as separated beings, and place nature in antithesis to the mind, as object to subject, thing to thought, death to life'.

Coleridge had perhaps Bentham and the utilitarians in mind.[14]

A society guided by 'substantial knowledge' is one which has passed through the process of cultivation – the agricultural root-meaning palpitating within the metaphor. But for Coleridge, culture is not instrumental: it is not to be pursued in the interests of something else, of international prestige or the encouragement of tourism, of the creation of jobs. He sees it as a human need in itself. Cultivation is a necessary prerequisite of civilization.

For Coleridge, cultivation was a moral activity founded in the imaginative and creative. It was an extension of the very processes of perception. There were several layers operating within the Coleridgean view of imagination, starting with the *fancy*, the crudest, the closest to mere memory. Primary imagination was in fact 'the living Power and prime Agent of all human perception ... a repetition in the finite mind of the eternal act of creation'. The poet's work operated at this most refined layer, the primary imagination. That function was the kernel of the workings of all art, and evoked, or in some sense continued or repeated, the original divine intervention in chaos.[15]

The notion of the arts as a single phenomenon – the plural unity – was employed in the years of the romantic movement, but without implying a decided and limited list of art-forms. The *Beaux Arts* as proclaimed by d'Alembert in Diderot's *Encyclopédie* were painting, sculpture, architecture, poetry and music, and this five-fold assemblage of arts had spread to other countries even before the French Revolution. But there was no implied sense of the relationships and dependencies that provide the plural notion of the Arts, with its more stationary definition and its openness to freshly arriving arts.

The linkages between the arts, their mutual proximities, have been subject to constant alteration. We think of poetry and painting as quite separate and unconnected skills, but a few generations ago they were felt to be much closer – since painting, sculpture and decorative art all derived their subject matter from the same great works of the poets and from the same Biblical texts. But Plato had regarded poetry, dance and music as essentially the same thing, and ever since the Pythagorean discovery of the numerical basis of musical intervals, music and mathematics were traditionally treated as a single set of propositions. The poetry-painting connection is still evident in much Victorian painting, which continued to concern itself with the re-expression in narrative terms of Bible and classic text. Marriages and divorces between art-forms continue to take place. If you think of the formats that were pioneered in radio during the 1930s and 1940s, you see a moment when literature was brought into a new and closer relationship with music than had previously been the case. In the 1960s, poetry and jazz formed an understanding that led towards the foundation of the modern pop industry, in which poetry is inextricably tied to music.

In the eighteenth century, the decorative arts had come to achieve a much wider social recognition than ever before, and when the much bigger middle-class public of the nineteenth century came to support art, it tended to concentrate on the same rather narrow group of decorative professions. But although painting was rooted in the skills of the craftsman, its social status rose rapidly, abandoning the other crafts to their lower social status; these other decorative skills came to lose their aura and status as arts when manufacturing processes enveloped them. Indeed, all the many strands of industrial, economic and religious history have to be tracked to keep up with the constant groupings and decouplings among art-forms over the last century and a half.

One may find a current example in the pop video, a distinctly new art-form born in our own time, which has acquired its status as a form in its own right as a result of the special role it plays within the distribution system for popular music. It combines photography or cinematography with music, and has acquired a characteristic expressionism and a sub-textual allegiance to consumerist ideology – beneath its extreme theatrical subversiveness, it communicates as repetitively as a hymn its sub-cultish message to the young. It is a form as closely defined and yet as broad in its possibilities as a sonnet; almost everything about it proclaims the way it has emanated from an earlier economic need – that of selling pop records through television exposure. But one can today trace a whole movement in cinematic style – a kind of neo-mannerism – to the skills and the characteristic attitudes of the pop video. It fuses various earlier forms and gives expression to a number of fresh interdependencies between artistic skills.

One might look back at the way in which the skills of stained glass intersected with those of the fresco, or at the combination of skills which came together in manuscript illumination or the binding of books; an apt illustration would be the connections between epic and tapestry. Gardening was at various times listed among the major arts, and in the late twentieth century one can see perhaps how this might be returning as a significant practised form of art alongside the revival of Restoration architecture, combined with the current concern with ecology and a growing popular interest in design.

Some art-forms come and go with shifting ideologies. Pottery is a good example. It is simultaneously high art and low practical or machine craft. A newly fired pot bought in the streets of a Third World city might be displayed as art in a home, but not a pot designed for the kitchen utensil industry. Here the criterion is something to do with the need to sanctify the hand-made and relegate the mass-produced; the deep desire – with its quasi-sacral satisfactions – to privilege the work of individuals over that of machines.

Calligraphy has become a rare and specialized activity, replaced in the era of cinema, television, and advertising by computer-aided hi-tech graphics. The two have been driven apart and the connection between them has become invisible, so distinct are their technical means. And think of engraving, which in the eighteenth century was treated as a separate, specialized high-art activity, distinct from painting precisely because of its different technological base; it has slipped somewhat downwards in social esteem to become one of a range of graphic art forms, more usually a tool of illustration than of independent art, but in its historic heritage still revered as a form of fine art.

In the twentieth century we have had to work out a fresh set of attitudes towards the hierarchy of art-forms because of the sheer pervasiveness of mechanical reproduction. Printed forms can be limited in circulation and thus acquire a sense of uniqueness as objects. But cultural experiences transmitted electronically have no such stability and lose their aura or aureole, as Walter Benjamin explained. Reproduction or transmission without limitation and the general democratization of art have dissolved the painfully constructed hierarchies and pyramids of art forms. We seldom find ourselves discussing the question of which is the greatest art-form, which is the chief among the arts.

'Only the poet', says Philip Sidney, '... lifted up by the vigor of his own invention ... doth growe in effect another nature, in making things either better than Nature brought forth, or, quite a newe, from such as never were in Nature – all other arts and sciences are tied to nature.'[16] Sidney was by no means the first to place poetry at the head of a hierarchy. The argument went back to the ancients. The reaction of Goethe, for example, to the attempt to press the arts into a united and equal family was one of complete rejection; the arts could not be considered as a group. They are so different from one another in their aims and their systems of expression, he thought, that an affinity between them could only occur in the mind of an amateur, perhaps in the mind of a lay member of the public, but never in that of an artist, who must be concerned only with the special problems of his own skill.[17]

The attempt to establish a hierarchy died with the disappearance of hierarchies in the social and professional worlds. But it remained, of course, in education, where teachers struggle with the content of bulging syllabuses. It has remained too in the realm of government, as administrators and lobbyists have locked horns over the agreed limits of subsidy. The artists, in the course of their pursuit of their own skills, have turned more and more often to government.

The demand for state support of the arts, and the argument about it, has lasted virtually since the era of Coleridge and the romantics. The painter Benjamin Haydon started to campaign for government support of 'High Art' (by which he meant grand painting) while he happened to be in prison for debt in 1823. While painting the portraits of a series of politicians a decade later, he told them that the quality of a country's painting was a guide to the state of its cultural and moral health.[18] Lord Melbourne softened his attitude to Haydon's case somewhat when he was told that high performance in art would be to the benefit of a country's manufacturing. 'When will England learn,' says the Art Journal in 1851, 'that even for the purposes of commerce Art is useful – and that where the higher and nobler Arts are assiduously cultivated, the inferior and industrial ones are also sure to flourish?'[19] But it was Prime Minister Robert Peel, who had made his fortune by mechanizing the textile industry, who eventually accepted the argument for setting up, with government help, a school of design (which became the Royal College of Art in London). And it is through such impurities of political motive that the loaded agenda of expectations held of subsidized arts has steadily grown. In our own day, we look to the arts to assist tourism, to enhance diplomatic objectives, to help entrench the equalities of gender and ethnicity, to provide opportunities for people suffering deficiencies of physical ability, as well as to help advance the cause of good manufacturing design.

The pressures for public support of the arts continued unceasingly – from the campaigns of William Morris and John Ruskin, the establishment of municipal orchestras in Victorian cities, Bernard Shaw's demands for a National Theatre – until John Maynard Keynes finally established the Arts Council of Great Britain in the aftermath of the Second World War. But by this time, state patronage had grown up in a score of other European countries, alongside municipal, regional and private support. In the United States, the National Endowments for the Arts and the Humanities appeared during the Lyndon Johnson administration, laden with the misgivings of a society that looks for political malfeasance in any free gift of government, and which worries about any breach of the constitutional separation of church and state and about any subsidy of cultural activity by the state.

But the arts, led by music and theatre, had become part of the furnishings of new nationhood, an up-and-coming branch of the welfare state, and an activity that lay tantalizingly at the cusp of public and private sectors.

In 1910, the young Rupert Brooke gave a talk in his rooms at Cambridge in which he argued that, since few poets – not even Mr Kipling – could make a living from poetry alone, the government should provide a system of bursaries to keep poetry and the other arts flourishing. Brooke harangued his fellows to look on the bright side of the blow struck by Democracy against middle-class privilege:

> The influence of Democracy on the Arts from this point of view – the Public – need not be bad. To show that it is good and to make it better, it is most importantly our duty to welcome and aid all the new and wider movements that come with the growth of Democracy and the rise of the new generation.[20]

But the arts continue, nearly a century later, to pose one of the most complex and unresolved challenges of democracy: they had to be released from their citadel of class privilege, but every alteration in their scope brings a demand for further rearrangement of the unitary concept that has been passed down to us. If the arts are a civil right, then surely they should admit to their number the art-forms that are the most popular. But these – cinema and television in particular – are industrial technologies requiring large amounts of risk capital, and are practised not by individuals but by complex industries. In some societies, cinema was admitted to the pantheon, and politicians had to devise ways to allow it levels of subsidy likely to enable it to flourish. The Anglo-Saxon world has on the whole refused to accept the argument for cinema as an art and the aesthetic parallels which it entails – and thus the complex governmental burden of paying for it.

Instead, it has tried to cope with the demand that the arts compensate for all the other unresolvable dysfunctions of society: provision should be made for those who are through ethnic origin tied to different cultural traditions, or by physical disablement prevented from full participation, both as members of an audience and as practitioners of a form. Those who live at great distances from metropolitan centres require to be compensated through the support of touring ballets, operas, theatre, exhibitions.

Every known nostrum of democracy has manifested itself upon the arts in the course of the present century. Rupert Brooke's was a juvenile version of the voice of early twentieth-century middle-class guilt; and the case for state bursaries has gradually turned into an argument for the arts as a kind of social service, for artists and audiences alike.

But in making that move, the arts, forever at the margins, forever indignant, have also been expelled from their moral home. They are sitting out the twentieth century as the senior branch of an entertainment industry, struggling with others for government funds and treated as a sectional interest, a lobby, much more than as a source of moral value. The argument about their overall priority, and the relative priorities among their different forms, is complicated by the fact that the membership of the club of the arts is in constant flux. Where the ancient world questioned the position of, say, architecture as a 'liberal art', the twentieth century questions the suitability of, say, jazz or Hindu dance for subsidy. The 'arts', that strange unity contrived by social rather than aesthetic circumstances, have forsaken their artisanal roots and have relocated in a political force-field, where the argument over social rights and social obligations, political support and political duty, is formulated in a way that guarantees that it can never end.

THREE

Making Culture Prevail: Arnold's Vision and Television

What held the arts together as a group, distinct from other branches of knowledge, was that people had come to see them as intimately linked with the aesthetic sensibility, the same mental faculty. Thus they held on to a shared semi-sacral status.

There were still, of course, the other areas of knowledge that had anciently been described as 'arts', and these came to be thought of as emanations of other physical or cerebral skills. One result was that artists often found themselves searching for the criteria of their own usefulness, for forms of self-justification that gave them a more central position in a world increasingly dominated by mathematics, engineering, medicine, astronomy, productive and ratiocinative arts. By laying claim to this sort of usefulness, if only metaphorically, artists thought they would become more secure, and in more recent times also better able to command remuneration. And by possessing, in the shape of 'the arts', an institution of their own, they were in a position to express their role and their importance in a political sense, their status as the locus of some kind of overt or invisible power. The unitary conception of the arts was thus a typical outcome of Enlightenment thinking. We live with the consequences.

The arts became an institution, a lobby, a hobby, a branch of entertainment. In late Marxism they took their place in the 'super-structure', and thus turned into evidence of passing ideology where they had once been the mainstay of religious practice. For some, the arts came to act as a substitute faith, and artists became the lay priesthood of an abandoned religion – and they were treated with the same hushed and respectful marginality in school curricula, in government budgets, in career guidance, the interloper in crowded timetables.

These were the implications of the implied bargain between society and the arts seen as a unity. When a new activity lays claim to being an 'art' – cinema is a good current example – it is in effect asking to be given the same status and the same intellectual and political privilege as music, painting, sculpture. When cinema or television people complain that their industry is not being treated in this country or that as an art, they mean to analogize their activity with, say, painting. The assertion implies a certain claim to state support, monetary and otherwise, as well as to social prestige. In this talk I shall look at a new phenomenon of culture – broadcasting – which has entered society by a different route, as a technology and as an industry. It is in many ways typical of the art-forms of the industrial era in that it began with its institutional housing prepared for it, its own ready set of political foundations.

In one sense, no art exists without throwing up an institution. As soon as someone says, 'Here is a new kind of object or activity which must be perceived aesthetically', the next example of the same genre will be compared with the first one, and someone will be asked to state the criterion by which the two may be judged. A third person will dispute that the second can really be an example of the new genre because it fails to conform to certain precepts buried in the first example. A fourth will suggest that the examples be collected, documented and exhibited in a specially designated gallery. All will ask who is to pay for it, and in the ensuing argument someone will complain that the whole

[34]

genre is excessively popular with, and probably damaging to, the more vulnerable young and ought to be under official regulation. Any product of the imagination will possess a capacity to constrain others and lead to argued comparisons. That is the beginning of institutionalization. A body of elected officers, a committee and a grant follow at later stages. Academies and institutes spring up to mediate and protect, to exalt, to sanitize.

Herbert Marcuse and other gurus active during the 1960s left us feeling thoroughly guilty about having any truck with official or self-appointed bodies. Their subtly repressive character seemed to be their only quality.[1] Foucault saw all modern societies as instruments of intense and increasing repression; prisons and law-courts, schools and hospitals – there existed around society a perimeter wall of state institutions, all of them struggling to defeat the impulses of humanity.[2] The family was also seen as one of those repressive institutions, and in case anyone could see a chink of light in this asphyxiating darkness – to which those advancing the description were miraculously immune – the oxymoron of repressive tolerance was invented to fill the gap.

The attack on institutions delivered by the Left of thirty years ago was only one further round in a long debate. Around art and letters a comparable argument has raged over the course of the centuries. At the time of the founding of the Royal Academy, Sir Joshua Reynolds said in defence of this new institution something to the effect that rules functioned like a suit of armour – they adorned the strong and only crippled the weak who tried to wear them. Only men of no genius find rules to be fetters, he said.[3] The Academy itself, founded in 1768, was not without its more ancient progenitors and forebears: Charles I had founded a Museum with something of the purposes of the Academy in 1636, at about the same time as the establishment of the

[35]

Académie in Paris. The Royal Academy was founded by a group of well-established artists who wanted to raise the status of their profession, to encourage appreciation on the part of the public, to set up a national school of art that would train future artists on the basis of sound principles, and to maintain a collection of exemplary work.[4]

Those have been among the purposes of all academies within the field of the arts ever since, and it is not difficult to see how such organizations can fall foul of the artists themselves. Many saw the Royal Academy as the ringleader of a stultifying conservatism, a block on creativity and progress; and something of that sentiment has hung around the portals of the Academy ever since, despite its self-transforming efforts in the 1930s to incorporate all the prevailing schools of British art. At the time of its founding in 1948, John Maynard Keynes held for the Arts Council of Great Britain the same aspiration to nourish the taste of the public and make the products of artists more generally accessible. The Council, which acquired in succeeding decades a tremendous, all-encompassing power of patronage across a great swathe of the arts, acquired more of the original roles of the Royal Academy, in the sense that it has helped to support the influence of leading groups within each art-form, while labouring to educate the public and make the arts more available geographically and socially. One inevitable outcome is that each art-form, as it enters the funding privilege, acquires a micro-bureaucracy of its own, a body of representative spokespersons, a pattern of funded organizations within the art-form.

What is different about the twentieth century's organization of culture is that it is founded upon more *social* ideals than the academies of earlier times. Where those academies were analogized in the minds of their founders perhaps with medieval guilds and patent-holding companies, the institutions of this century feel their natural analogues to be the new social services, health, education, the police, social welfare. They are concerned with the business of provisioning the aesthetic larder of society. In Britain there persists a faint echo of rationing, a pattern of comforting austerity. In the United States, the 1927 Radio Act which set up the Federal Communications Commission to regulate American broadcasting (renewed as the Communications Act of 1934), speaks of 'public interest, convenience, necessity', terms strongly evocative of the era of the New Deal.[5]

In the public documents that deal with cultural matters, including radio and television, one can often detect something being held back, leashed, restrained. And to see how broadcasting came to acquire its special kinds of restraining institution, amid an unending debate about itself, one must look for clues among earlier debates – which prepared the public policies long before the birth of the technology itself.

In his final lecture as Oxford Professor of Poetry in 1867, Matthew Arnold had established a new paradigm for the diffusion of culture. In a paper called 'Sweetness and Light', which became part of his book *Culture and Anarchy*, Arnold traces his own inspiration and the origins of this now-familiar phrase to two German writers, Lessing and Herder: 'Because they humanised knowledge; because they broadened the basis of life and intelligence; because they worked powerfully to diffuse sweetness and light.'[6] This is the voice of Arnold the school inspector; not the voice of a missionary so much as that of a civil servant, someone seeking to establish a policy and make it work – or 'prevail', to use one of Arnold's favourite words.

In Arnold's most-quoted paragraph about the diffusion of culture, there is a powerful sense of zeal, penetrated by the natural egalitarianism of the educator:

This is the *social* idea; and the men of culture are the true apostles of equality. The great men of culture are those who have had a passion for diffusing, for making prevail, for carrying from one end of society to the other, the best knowledge, the best ideas of their time; who have laboured to divest knowledge of all that was harsh, uncouth, difficult, abstract, professional, exclusive; to humanise it, to make it efficient outside the clique of the cultivated and learned, yet still remaining the best knowledge and thought of the time, and a true source, therefore, of sweetness and light.[7]

Every phrase sends a beam forward to the language of the institutionalization of early broadcasting – including that unmistakable note of spiritual pride. Those are the sentiments that animated not only the BBC, but also the Workers' Educational Association, the British Film Institute, the Arts Council of Great Britain. They had come down to Arnold through, amongst others, J. H. Newman, who had 'laid it down' in *On the Scope and Nature of University Education* that 'the culture of the intellect is a good in itself and its own end ... as the body may be tended, cherished, and exercised with a simple view to its general health, so may the intellect also be generally exercised in order to its perfect state; and this *is* its cultivation.'[8] Here, Newman is echoing Coleridge in his use of the word 'cultivation', and thus re-emphasizing his opposition to the utilitarian view that men should be educated in order to perform certain kinds of work. Within every class, thought Arnold, there existed a small body of people who are somehow outside the dominant *mores* of their class, who are infected with the humane spirit, what he calls 'the love of human perfection'. Another key term used of this group is 'the best self'. It is this small body of people spread through the classes of society who are able to evoke, through education and art, the 'best self' in others of their respective classes, and thus establish standards within 'the fermenting mind of the nation'.

For Arnold, the role of the state in achieving such a purpose was to behave as a 'centre of authority and light'. But the state had become the self-protective agency of the aristocracy (whom Arnold called, though playfully, the Barbarians); the middle classes (Arnold called these the Philistines) were wanting to undermine the state; while the working-class (Arnold called these the Populace) 'had long lain half-hidden amidst its poverty and squalor' and was starting to assert its privileges, listed by Arnold as 'doing as he likes ... marching where it likes, meeting where it likes, bawling what it likes, breaking what it likes ... All this, I say, tends to anarchy.'[9] Culture, therefore, represents as a kind of salvation. It goes beyond hatred and has 'one great passion, for sweetness and light'. The word becomes elevated beyond any of its available meanings to occupy a position in Arnold's thought comparable to that of Charity in St Paul's. It slips towards an abstract usage (Raymond Williams quotes Frederic Harrison's unkind jibe about Arnold: 'This same ... *sauerkraut* or culture'[10]), but it is a secular abstraction. Culture functions in a social world and, in the form of sweetness and light, it has a positive, almost *administrative*, role to play in the context of its special relationship with the State. Culture could reduce the tensions between classes in what had become a deeply divided society, but it would also ensure that the 'Populace' found its due place within the existing social order.

Fifty years later, Sir John Reith was to write, while improvising a justification for public service broadcasting: 'Broadcasting is a servant of culture and culture has been called the study of perfection.' The last phrase is lifted directly from Arnold, who indeed called culture the 'study of perfection', but had added, 'a harmonious perfection, developing all sides of our humanity; and as general perfection, developing all parts of our society'.[11]

Fifty years later still, in 1977, the Annan Report on the Future of Broadcasting contained further references to Arnoldian 'sweetness and light', but this time in the context of a statement that the ideals of Arnoldian middle-class culture were hard to accommodate to the demands of the 1960s.[12]

The birth of radio in the United States was not accompanied by exactly the same hopes or policies, but in the diversity of the cultural opportunities it offered its accomplishments were not negligible – in the early years at least. Its extreme commercialism baffled travellers from Britain and played some part in the battle to ensure the BBC monopoly. The BBC presented an orderly alternative to the American radio scene, with its suddenly emerging networks, the fierce competition to cover national events, and the endless fight for advertising revenue. Reith held a meeting with the incredulous bosses of the new CBS radio network and explained that the BBC looked beyond momentary public tastes and interests, considering that it had a responsibility to help shape them. The 'supply of good things will create a demand for them,' explained Sir John, 'not waiting for the demand to express itself'.[13]

America was more pessimistic than Britain about the possibilities of mass society. Walter Lippmann thought that democracy was coming under strain because of the sheer impossibility of ensuring that citizens acquired the knowledge of affairs necessary to uphold the system.[14] In Britain, the leader of the new documentary film movement, the Scot John Grierson, saw in radio and cinema the instrument of the renewal of democracy. Sir Norman Angell continued to express the belief, in the early 1920s, that better education was a practical way to ensure that political disorder did not overwhelm the public mind.[15] In conditions of peace, greater social justice could be obtained by reforming the education system and thereby forcing the press lords to elevate the style and content of the popular newspapers.

The radio broadcasting of the era was suffused with this kind of practical optimism: broadcasters spoke of a common culture through which the discourses of public life would be opened up to a mass public, together with access to the resources of cultural life previously locked away for a privileged élite. Radio saw its social role as a counterbalance to the intellectual depredations of Lord Northcliffe's and Lord Harmsworth's newspapers. This was in significant contrast to the condition of radio in the United States, where religious broadcasts by charismatic priests seemed to take precedence over broadcasting designed to educate listeners in public affairs, though not exclusively so. The hundreds of stations offered a tremendous variety of programmes and held out Utopian promises: in 1921, a new programme journal promised that, with the new medium, 'government will be a living thing to its citizens instead of an abstract and unseen force.'[16] But Secretary of Commerce Hoover was reluctant to do more than criticize the gathering tendency towards excessive advertising. He publicly deprecated 'the use of radio broadcasting for direct sales effort', but then conceded that the industry itself should decide what to do about advertising, 'not ... Government compulsion and legislation'.[17]

The shaping processes of American broadcasting, its practical assimilation into American society, were carried out by the industry and taken out of the hands of the legislators, who have never in effect regained their power over the medium. The kind of discussion which had enveloped broadcasting in Britain – and which, despite all that has happened in the 1980s, has never ceased – rapidly evaporated in the United States. In the 1920s there was a much greater overlap between the varieties of radio offered in the two systems than is customarily recalled, but the control of American radio, from Congress and the Federal Communications Commission downwards, was buried in utterly different discourses, notably those connected with revenue, competition, technical efficiency. To be sure, some of the topics were the same. An argument about monopoly took place on both sides of the Atlantic, in America to shun it, but in Britain to welcome it as a way of guaranteeing the Arnoldian vision. Monopoly was justified as the means to make culture 'prevail' in the new medium; in America it was rejected, not only because it was unacceptable to the morality of industry, but because it seemed to be the path to totalitarianism.

The establishment of an organized radio medium in Britain took place at a moment, in the aftermath of a world war, when Arnoldian ideas were being revived. The BBC had a notion of cultural equality built into it. Indeed, the terms BBC and cultural equality were almost a tautology. In the United States, by contrast, it was a moment when the long-standing American dilemma over the meanings of equality in constitutional terms was being overtaken by an intensified drive towards economic competition. It was only much later, during the renewed panic about education in post-Korean War America, that real thought was given to establishing a form of publicly funded, educative television – and by this time, public service broadcasting found itself not only in conflict with established audience taste and public policy, but also with vast established commercial interests. The kind of link that held between Matthew Arnold and John Reith did not run through the America of corporations. The regulatory discourse of America was not without misgivings about the commercial nature of the medium – the *locus classicus* being the frequently quoted remarks of Herbert Hoover about 'drowning a great public service in advertising chatter'.[18]

But in America, egalitarianism came out in the national campaigns against racism, in arguments about mass education and, much more recently, in arguments about gender, ethnicity, disablement. In the United Kingdom, such figures as Coleridge, Newman, Arnold and Mill had established a concern for forms of cultural egalitarianism that constantly recurs thereafter in the writings of Raymond Williams, Richard Hoggart and many others. In the minds of some, it has been a cause which, as it was for Arnold, is more important than the struggle over class. Radio broadcasting during wartime provided the clearest and most consistent, though temporary, expression of this.

Arnold had not been talking into a vacuum. He flourished during the golden age of Victorian journalism, when there had been two distinct parties contending for political power. A well-to-do entrepreneur and a skilled journalist could get together and produce a profitable daily journal, whether in the Liberal or the Conservative interest. Social conflicts were expressed within that duality, and supposedly held in check by it. But as the century closed, the economic logic of the newspaper industry altered; a 'nationalization' of politics took place, which built a new formation of political life upon the broader social classes rather than the narrower political groups. The vocabulary of the newspaper was forced to broaden under the resulting pressure from new ranges of readers. The polite symmetry of classes to which Arnold had playfully attached his Barbarian and Philistine labels no longer obtained, and the change-over was symbolized in the rise of the halfpenny press. This replaced the penny press of the mid-Victorian era, a press that had symbolized social respectability and, in retrospect, seemed to have acted as the guarantor of political stability.[19]

In America, the Hearst press reflected a parallel set of trends at work in the dominant popular medium of the time. In the

1880s, Pulitzer's *World* was somewhat similar to W. T. Stead's *Pall Mall Gazette*, pioneering the vulgarities of the 'interview' and covering sensational stories and sporting events. In France, where *Le Petit Parisien* achieved historic levels of circulation, voices were raised to condemn the worsening quality of daily journalism – voices which raised the accusation, for the first time, of 'Americanization'.

In the late nineteenth century a communications revolution took place, brought on by progress in mass education and by the rise of new technology, paralleled by an increase in personal disposable wealth and the growing market for advertising. Around this grew an increasing sense of nationhood, a metropolitanization of politics paralleled by a growing distrust of politics, all fuelled by the prevailing journalistic forms. The most significant change noted by politicians in the content of the new mass newspapers was the diminution in the expression of opinions; news grew in scope as the techniques for collecting it and presenting it grew more spectacular. The democracy that was emerging was quite different from what Arnold had predicted, and hoped for.

From the 1920s onwards, widespread concern about the influence of the press over the mass mind led to the setting-up of a series of commissions of enquiry both in Britain and the USA. These marked the turning-points in the evolution of public doctrines about journalism and its values, doctrines that attempted to express and enforce notions of objectivity and social responsibility. Within the newspaper press, a seemingly endless dialogue, often acrimonious, broke out between governments and press barons. A succession of voices in Europe, America and Britain demanded control of press concentration, control of journalistic training, the establishment of official bodies to investigate the newly identified crimes of public expression.

Labour and Conservative newspapers had both flourished in the decades before 1900, but for the next seventy years there were constant complaints from an anguished Labour Party that, despite its vast popular following, it suffered the injustice of finding no niche in the newspaper market for a commercially viable title of its own. The newspaper, which had once symbolized stability, access, respectable control, now became a battlefield of public values. Some thought that within a private-sector press there could never again be fairness of coverage, the level playing field for the competitive struggles of political opinion, and certainly no real opportunity for new entrepreneurs to enter the competition and hold their own.

The founders of broadcasting were wary of creating public institutions, whether regulatory or organizational, that reflected and amplified this kind of political imbalance. They all devised formulae to express the sense of promised fairness, but also bound the medium to maintain what were regarded as necessary standards in both morals and culture. It was obvious that these would be harder to guarantee if and when the broadcasting managers were pursuing commercial ends. All framers of modern broadcasting constitutions have oscillated between the idea of a public service which, in effect, pursues the policy of 'making prevail' a certain set of values or standards and, on the other hand, the idea of a market of information and entertainment, based upon nostalgic recall of the nineteenth-century newspaper industry. Both ideas undergo recurrent reinterpretation and reappear with fresh purposes and justifications in the academy or in public life. In the late twentieth century, both options remain, in pure and mixed forms, and the doctrines that underpin them float in and out of favour, from country to country.

The 1980s saw a successful revival of free-market thinking, encouraged by the rapid collapse of Communism, and both

Britain and America pushed through market-orientated reforms of their broadcasting systems. Each sought to reduce regulation and release the managers of the multiplying forms of broadcasting from as many prohibitions and inhibitions as possible. In both cases, the object was to encourage domestic companies to make a better showing in the international market for television programmes and other services related to the new information technologies. Many other countries underwent comparable changes, and for the same reasons: to hasten the development of a modern information infrastructure that would keep the country concerned competitive in what has become a global market. In the USA, Mark Fowler (chairman of the Federal Communications Commission, the regulatory agency, during the 1980s) and his Chief Legal Assistant wrote a widely discussed paper in the *Texas Law Journal* setting out a strong case for the market-place approach.[20] I should explain that Mr Fowler was the gentleman widely quoted at the time as having called television just 'another household appliance – a toaster with pictures'. *Time* magazine had called him the 'evangelist of the market-place'. But even the *Texas Law Review* article agreed that there was a case for publicly funded television in certain circumstances – children's television was instanced. 'Economists have long recognised the existence of "merit goods", which society values although the marketplace cannot explain or justify their retention.'

The market has always been seen as the guarantor of free expression as well as of good practice in industrial regulation. But broadcasting has revealed problems and opportunities that seemed to justify a consistent making of exceptions. But in the mood of the 1980s, regulation was seen as a problem, no longer as a solution. The Federal Communications Commission was castigated as the last of the New Deal dinosaurs, a survivor of

Roosevelt's attempts to use public institutions and funds to solve the problems of mass society. Its rules enforcing Equal Time in matters of controversy were jettisoned.[21]

In Britain, the Peacock Committee[22] wrestled with the problem of how, if at all, to reconcile the obligations of maintaining high standards with those of competing in the new market-place of electronic information. It concluded that technology was now rapidly bringing about a vast increase in the supply of channels, which would in time make possible a system of subscription for chosen channels and payments per programme viewed. Technology was thus reversing the paradigm of broadcasting, by which channels were scattered, were 'broad-cast' through a magnetic realm that was by its nature scarce and necessarily so. But the writers of the Peacock Report agreed with Mr Fowler of the Federal Communications Commission that there could be sections of the programme range which the market-place and advertising would not reach – the 'merit goods' – and that these could only be saved by a public body, funded by government, that would subsidize otherwise-commercial institutions to create and supply them. One hears the echo in both American and British examples of an Arnoldian 'making prevail', a necessity to ensure the universality of certain elements of the traditional 'high' culture.

In the 1990s, pendulums have been swinging back. The views of the German writer Jürgen Habermas have spread, establishing the idea that the media of modern times have created what he calls the 'public sphere', a neutral zone through which relevant information passes and which by its nature is free from control by the state.[23] It is an arena of rational argument which the participants enter on an equal basis, their ideas and their argument amplified through the media. In a way, the Habermasian vision is that of the small eighteenth-century American community, or an idealized version of John Stuart Mill's Victorian London. It is an optimistic image of the media society, and one that could perhaps only have emerged in modern Germany; for in Germany, the new constitution gave firm expression to the priority of regional over federal responsibility for all matters of culture, with active provincial political participation and public ownership of channels. But the Habermasian vision is attractive, to the academy of Western societies at least, even where a large sector of the media is in private hands. He has perhaps noticed something that prevailing pessimism had caused the academy to overlook. His writings are to an extent reminiscent of those of John Dewey and the 'Progressive' movement in the United States, who saw in the coming generation of communication technologies a fresh device for creating the lost sense of American community in the era following rapid urbanization.[24]

One crucial text that reveals 1990s thinking is the British government's 1994 *Future of the BBC*, issued by the Department of National Heritage. Its oxymoron subtitle, 'Serving the Nation – Competing World-wide',[25] neatly expresses the problem and suggests the difficulty of the solution. In the 1920s, radio seemed to be the ideal, the God-given technology of culture for giving expression to the Arnoldian zeal for 'making prevail'. In the 1990s, technological change is the seemingly inexorable cause of the older ideology having become unsustainable. The changes in economic doctrine are adduced as an additional confirming reason. But at the same time, there is a growing fear of what might happen to the schedule of programmes if public service broadcasting were to disappear. What would happen to free time for election programmes? What would happen to high-quality drama and entertainment, the mainstays of Britain's export trade in television? It is this secondary wave of anxieties that is causing government in Britain, and elsewhere in Europe, to ask itself again whether the auctioning of franchises and hour-by-hour competition between terrestrial, cable and satellite channels is really the inevitable outcome of irresistible forces in technological history. The 1994 White Paper makes it clear that the public service, even if its channels necessarily come to account for only a fraction of the total programme material available, may yet turn out to be a necessary long-term safety net of standards and quality, however these are defined.

By the turn of the century, five hundred channels of moving images will be on offer in Europe alone, mostly via one of the new technologies. In addition, there are the new types of video game that now supply a large proportion of the narrative culture, and there will be new forms of digital transmission that will render the potential supply of fantasy and factual material infinite. Much of it can no longer be policed, let alone licensed. A large proportion of it is material that would never be permitted access to an audience by the regulatory system that has existed since the birth of radio and television. The shoring-up of demoralized public service broadcasting is a safety measure, accepted only reluctantly by some of the politicians concerned. But in the context of myriad freely flowing commercial channels, many of them completely acceptable by traditional canons, it is hard to see how in Britain, for example, the BBC or the Independent Television Commission regulatory agency can between them maintain hegemony over standards and quality. In the new context, public service broadcasting can only set examples; it cannot make them prevail.

But what are the standards that seem salient at this point in broadcasting history? It is interesting to compare those now advanced by government in Britain, in the 1994 White Paper, with those advanced a decade ago by the Broadcasting Research Unit, an outright lobbyist for the public service idea, led by

Professor Richard Hoggart.[26] The government lists ten objectives, and of these, eight were put forward by the Broadcasting Research Unit. The ten are: serving viewers' interests, serving a diversity of often minority audiences, reflecting the national identity, supporting the arts, aiming at high quality, including creativity and originality, maintaining editorial independence, appealing to a variety of social groups throughout the geographical area of the country, placing an emphasis on training and research, giving good value for the licence fee, and becoming more fully accountable for activities and expenditure.

This account is remarkable for its consistency, despite the changes of the last decade. It is hard to detect any really important change since the 1920s, except for an increased emphasis on the BBC as a kind of international showpiece – and, of course, the statements designed to put pressure on the BBC to expand its commercial activities at home and abroad. There exists a large global market that was absent even a decade ago, and the BBC is urged to enter this, though without prejudicing its special domestic responsibilities or using the licence fee as a subsidy for its overseas commercial operations. Another area of fresh commitment is the requirement that the BBC should work within the new pan-national, pan-institutional project, the Citizen's Charter, under which the BBC would make open promises to its audiences about its content and mode of operation, and become far more accessible to suggestion and complaint. But of course it can no longer hope to maintain its share of the viewing audience, and the expectation held of it in the mid-1990s by the White Paper is that it should prepare its schedules so as to ensure that every viewing family watches its channels at least once a week. The BBC itself has said that it hopes to maintain a constant 30 per cent share of the viewing audience. But as it looks ever more closely at that audience, it seems to shatter into dozens of smaller groups, classes, genders, ethnicities, categories of hobbyist, all subject to the competitive blandishments of equally specialized satellite or cable channels. The social vision precedes the sociological vision, so highly speciated that it becomes inaccessible to a culture addressed to a whole society.

What can be said of the relationship of broadcasting today as a cultural or economic good, as a contributor to the good life or the quality of citizenship? We know that, throughout the world, the average person spends about half of his or her freely disposable time watching the television screen, the young and the old in particular. In the debate of the 1980s, the term 'quality' was used to head the agenda because quality offered transportable and comprehensible criteria by which to judge the social value of a non-transactional public service activity. But 'quality' can also be taken to mean the superimposition of values upon the actual tastes and demands of the audience. Quality can slip into being simply a judgement by the market. It can also be the Trojan Horse of patrician or socially manipulating interests. Quality can also be used to cover a range of considerations reserved by, and coded by, the professionals for themselves – today a large proportion of producers are small businesses, anxious about profit margins, markets, subsidiary sales. Nor can judgements of quality be left exclusively to audiences (to 'consumer sovereignty'), since that would subject questions of social value to those of first-level personal choice. Quality can therefore no longer be treated as synonymous with producer freedom, or with managerial predilection, or with audience preference. Quality now demands a new constituency if it is to have stable meaning.

Perhaps the term 'quality' has just run out of steam as a terminological resource for dealing with the trying complexities of the issues involved. Perhaps in this age of multiple choices our culture has lost the ability to make that set of judgements that once seemed so easy. Perhaps quality is an atavistic throwback to the old hierarchy of the arts, which enjoyed an extended lease of life as part of an Anglo-Saxon class fix. Running through the whole dilemma is the fact that a large section of the entire output of moving images and broadcast sound – and all the adjuncts to these – is now indeed fully commodified and subjected to the economics of markets. Broadcasting is not the only function of society now reduced to this dualism; health services are also offered into a quasi-privatized, commoditized and accountable market. The discussion is muddied by the fact that every supplier of every kind of service now claims to represent the interests of the consumer, and to be fully accountable in respect of quality and standards.

One current writer who tackles this issue head-on is Pierre Bourdieu. He begins by bringing out the distinctions between what he calls the 'naïve gaze', or popular aesthetic, and the 'pure' or 'aesthetic' gaze of the sophisticated viewer.[27] The two approach the medium of television with distinct purposes in mind, the latter deliberately wanting to distance itself from the former. To use cultural forms in search of social markers is the convention in, say, opera and gallery painting, but in television it tends towards a kind of distortion. Television's function as the generator and reflector of national spectacle and pageantry – great sporting and solemn political events – is separable from the dilemma of style, except in so far as the medium acts as the inventor or shaper of much of this material. The removal of these events from the universal gaze through the purchase of rights by cable and satellite operators poses a massive challenge to the public service idea, and indeed to the whole proposition of nationhood and national culture. But the problem also bears upon the shifting nature of 'quality'. For television is a normative activity, even when the vast audiences of past history are split into fragments. In a competitive system, public service television has to have privileged access to the major icons of its society, to the pageantry of politics and sport, if it is not to fail in its basic function. It cannot be left with partial or random access to this range of meaning-creating material.

But if television neglects to satisfy Bourdieu's 'aesthetic' gaze and falls back on acting only as a service to the popular culture, whether or not at a high level of professional skill, then it fails again in its universalizing duties. The argument of Bourdieu perhaps carries further in France than Britain, for in Britain every sector, every ethnic group and class, looks to see itself reflected in the crystal of television, as a form of recognition within the polity. The American writer James Carey puts the point by drawing attention to an idea of Dewey, that we should replace the 'transmission' view of culture with the 'ritual' view, and that all the cognate meanings of this central concept should be brought into active semantic play: communicate, communion, community – for all of these point to an inherent human need for cultural phenomena to be used to associate people, to offer common experiences.[28]

James Carey points to the linkage between the models of culture we employ in the television age and the physical condition of our society. We have ended up using each new advance in communications technology 'in terms of their potential for economics and politics'; our cities have thus become the domains of bureaucracy and technology rather than places to live. Houses, streets, roads have undergone their twentieth-century redesigns simply to facilitate commercial and technological possibilities and the forms of government they appear to require. Our current fascination with communication reflects what is a *derangement* in our view of the world. 'We are almost always coerced by our traditions,' writes Carey, 'into seeing [society] as a network of power, administration, decision and control – as a political order. Alternatively ... as an economic order.'[29] But of course social life is more than politics and economics; it possesses a repressed ritual order, consisting of moral and religious, personal and aesthetic dimensions, which are being, and in effect have now become, systematically expunged. The *practical* has been redefined merely as that which most immediately satisfies the most urgent requirements of government and commerce in technological mode. To ask what it is one wants to 'prevail' in our inhabited world necessitates interrogation of the accepted division between what the market deems to be romantic and what the intellectual deems to be practical; it means discovering how to reconstruct a democracy of society's real needs – together with the restoration of the necessary language with which to express these in widely accepted terms.

In the last decade, many of the arguments employed in the television debate, as in other contemporary issues, have switched hands from left to right or from right to left. Rupert Murdoch often accuses the advocates of public service broadcasting of being merely self-serving intellectuals, exercising a debilitating influence on society, obsessed with class distinctions and refusing to move with the times. But that is pretty well what the left used to say about the BBC and the IBA in the 1960s and 1970s. The left in British politics used to condemn the licence fee as an unredeemable and regressive poll tax, and wanted to substitute a direct, annual government grant. Today, the argument for the retention of the licence fee tends to be heard from the left, because the system contains some vestige of the social vision that once inspired the management of broadcasting.

On the political right, perhaps still inspired by the Peacock Report, one hears a 1990s case for direct government subsidy to eke out advertising in a fully commercial system. Here, government support for quality programmes is seen as the price of abolishing the BBC. But there is a real problem confronting those who support the complete privatization of television, cable, satellite and terrestrial services: the marginal cost of supplying terrestrial and satellite television services is very close to zero, for once the transmitter is switched on, additional viewers and listeners cost the supplier nothing; the cost of linking up an additional cable viewer in a street already supplied with a cable is similarly very low. Looked at from the point of view of consumer benefit, it would seem more effective to offer a universal service for a fixed payment, equalized among users, than to sell the same services to a small fraction of the audience, a viewer at a time. And there are other differences with television seen as pure commodity: television programmes – rather like second-hand cars – can only be judged and reduced to consumer choice retrospectively, since viewers have only the vaguest 'brand image' of the supplying organization to go on when deciding how to allocate their time between programmes. With such a commodity, the supplier has little incentive to invest more than is necessary to make the first sale – the temptation is always to make a sale and move on. Thus, many audiences in countries where television has been privatized – France is a good example – end up deeply regretting the change and feeling cheated. The market fails to produce that constant pressure for improvement which occurs when the buyer depends upon the brand name of a continuing supplier.

Of course, every decade throws up a different set of needs; and new frustrations arise to set the frontier for reform. By the 1970s, the broadcasting institutions which had brought the new television culture of the 1960s into existence seemed suddenly to stand remote and inaccessible, like ancient abbeys awaiting the

Reformation. Television production was simply a skill contained within these institutions, and no one outside them seemingly had any right to suggest, to complain, let alone actually to contribute to the medium. It had become the dominant means of political communication, but only the direct employees of the channels could make programmes for a public. At that time, the reform demanded was 'access' to the air, some diminution of the monopoly power of the institutions; there had emerged a new series of political and social concerns, a generational 'new politics', and there existed a cohort who wanted a place where they could use the most powerful available means of communication for themselves. It all seems very obvious today, but twenty years ago 'access' felt as if it were the key not only to the open making of video images but also to a wider agenda of liberation.

But today the problem is more one of how the medium might be made to link people, to express a common citizenship among nations, and especially within nations, to re-create the sense of identity. Parents want television to assist in the processes of parenthood; teachers want to use television as a means of expression and to show how a society creates meaning. One widespread fear is that the competition for audiences and the cheapness of programmes bought in the now-mature international market will squeeze the local, the national, the *authentic*, out of mainstream television, thus intensifying the sense of alienation. The reform frontier has moved a great distance in twenty years.

In his essay *Two Concepts of Liberty,* Isaiah Berlin opens up the great gap of meaning between those who want liberty in order to curb authority – some of the pro-market theorists of the present might come in this category – and those who want, through liberty, authority placed in their own hands.[30] In the latter camp one might place some of those whose concern is to enforce the new shibboleths of political correctness. Both views are active within the debate over the future of television. The pro- and anti-regulation camps illustrate the two kinds of libertarian. Berlin sees the two not as different interpretations of a single concept of liberty, but rather as 'divergent and irreconcilable attitudes to the ends of life'. The claims of each sound absolute, are absolute, but, as he concludes, 'each has an equal right to be classed among the deepest interests of mankind'. Berlin quotes an admired but unnamed contemporary as saying: 'To realise the relative validity of one's convictions and yet stand for them unflinchingly, is what distinguishes a civilised man from a barbarian.' Certainly, in the context of the broadcasting debate the different kinds of libertarian have accepted the relative validity of their claims. Complete privatization of this dominant, and now abundant, means of culture is as impossible and undesirable as complete regulation in pursuit of quality. Both camps know that.

Where concepts of culture have dissolved into a series of relativities, there exists no point from which the pressure for a 'making prevail' can be exerted. There are too many meanings attached to democracy for there to be a point at which to pivot, to regulate, the rapidly proliferating technological apparatus of culture. There is no still point for a turning world. For acceptance of the degree of authority necessary for a 'making prevail', there has to exist some quantum of consent in language, in ethics, in a canon of materials. Broadcasting presents the stark logic of a wider issue. If you are seeking the modern canon of the arts, the universally accepted texts, you have to look to the international market. The airport lounge is our canonic architecture. Japanese design in cars and household goods offers us our canonic art. American soap opera is our canonic fiction. Those are the great wells of common allusion in a world of nations subject to a global economy. Those have become the materials of shared meaning. And the progress of that economy is the continued working-through of the great victory of Reason, which brought us the unitary, secularized, professionalized conception of the arts which I described at the beginning. To reverse the powerful secularizing logic of the Enlightenment is indeed what T.S. Eliot meant when he wrote: 'Prophesy to the wind, to the wind only, for only the wind will listen.'[31] And how apt that the biographer of John Reith adopted those lines as the epigraph for the life of that visionary founder of a remarkable service of broadcasting.[32] For, to the generations born between the 1920s and the 1970s, the disappearance of the public places and public spaces on which public service broadcasting was built symbolizes the disintegration of the moral housing of the political world. The cultural consequences of the loss of that institutional power would be incalculable. That is why, if forced to guess, I would predict that public service broadcasting will find a painful way back in the aftermath of the technological upheavals of the present decade. Reconstructing the terms of its authority and the guarantees of its resources will have to be the task of another cohort.

FOUR

Information as Paradigm of Culture

Sometimes an Idea bursts upon the world with the imperative of a hurricane. So many issues appear to be simultaneously illuminated by it that there seem to be no others remaining to be clarified, and for a time the unresolved issues are indeed obscured by a haze of associated terminology, much of it applied by analogy. Think of the arrival of cybernetics, or of Heisenberg's Uncertainty Principle, or earlier, of the Freudian idea of the existence of the Unconscious.

The new Idea rapidly invades every science, and its analogues and derivative images spread through the arts and into political discourse, eventually arriving at the gates of government. The Idea becomes both paradigm and catch-phrase. It is used in advertising. It becomes the heading of newspaper sections. It enters school curricula. In some sense, it alters our ways of conceptualizing the world. Soon it becomes difficult to remember or to re-imagine the discourses of the world that preceded the Idea. When the age of Freudian psychology dawned, people did not recall the complicated theories of phrenology; the Ptolemaic world disappeared from consciousness with the establishment of the Copernican. The mind-set alters. To call to mind the beliefs and attitudes that emanated from an ancient paradigm even a decade after it imploded is like looking at a city with the help of an ancient map. The world before has acquired a sepia tone.

The reason why certain new theories and their accompanying labels establish themselves so effectively is simply because sensitive people want to exploit them, to test the breadth of their validity; they want to be the first to brandish them, to digest them, to derive extensions and analogies, and in the end, of course, to abandon them and move on.

In our own time, we have seen the concept of culture – used, as indeed Eliot used it, to mean 'a whole way of life'[1] – penetrate the social sciences and acquire new uses in commerce, management, economics, politics. The term was long nurtured in anthropology, implying, in the phrase of Clifford Geertz, 'the accumulated totality of organised systems of significant symbols'.[2] An earlier anthropologist, Sir Edward Tylor, had listed its areas of salience more concisely: 'knowledge, belief, law, morals, customs'.[3] And it is culture, used in this widely encompassing but still precisely defined sense, that now plays so grand a role in modern political language. It suggests the repertoire of potential behaviours on which individuals draw to find their bearings in the world.

Another term which has played a similarly transforming role in our conception of the world, and of our individual roles within it, is ecology. It has become explanatory but also metaphorical, descriptive as well as normative, and today exercises its force ubiquitously in every area of knowledge as well as in every area of policy. Its use reflects the way we have become encouraged, or obliged, to think internationally in the post-imperial era. It summons up and summarizes in the user's mind a whole series of political concerns, sources of guilt, feelings of awe and respect for nature, rules of personal life.

The mathematical notion of chaos is another that has been acting out a kind of verbal catalysis in the world of ideas. Of more recent origin than the others I have mentioned, it is currently moving through the lexical highways, and with it is its companion concept, complexity.[4] These terms began almost as mathematical cults, illuminating and encouraging a group of early adherents who explore and summon up the creative potential of the thinking behind them. Like many of the notions I am alluding to, they soon pass through specialist journals and academic conferences and are taken up by the media. The specialist journalists and publicists extract pollen from the idea and start fertilizing other groups of potential subject enthusiasts. While each such idea, and its associated terminology, originates in one corner of the intellectual world, each has to carve out its own unique route through the landscape of the arts and sciences. Only in its later stages does it become an everyday term, and by this time it begins to turn to metaphor, the original force of the idea becoming slowly attenuated.

The new concept is taken up by people for whom the term seems to explain more than it does; but it does point up a number of issues. The analogies that are being spun from it go on to enjoy an influential life of their own; when they are used, they possess an aura of universal salience, they are revelatory. Chaos, for example, is a mathematical idea at present in mid-career, moving across the intellectual and imaginative horizon. The principal examples of its use have been derived, to great effect, from fields as far apart as weather forecasting and zoology; but it is already quite difficult to think about the fickleness of the weather without remembering that hard-working butterfly in China, whose flutterings might have caused today's hurricane; and equally hard to look at stock prices, or falling leaves in a forest, or tadpoles in a pond, without the transcending metaphors provided by chaos theory springing to mind. It passes from mathematical theory into the realm of poetic metaphor, then popular stock phrase, before reaching a condition of semantic stasis. It begins as a kind of shorthand and then becomes usable without the need actually to think the metaphor, without it necessarily turning into a mere word. We use it as an interim explanation of the inexplicability of the world before us.

Nowadays, a public person may talk about an exam culture or a poverty culture, hardly recalling the quasi-anthropological origins of that metaphorical usage. We talk about the ecology of industry, of the broadcasting system, of the retail market, the ecology of human manners, the ecology of the larder. And when we see any random scattering of objects or of data on a sheet of paper, we nowadays begin to wonder whether perhaps, in the chaos, elements of a vaster pattern might be discernible with the help of a computer. You see a stain on a carpet, and the chaos term *fractal* may spring to mind: poetry, conversation, popular cultural forms all begin to use the word or phrase as an image, to suggest further areas of salience. There, in the imaginative realm, we gain fresh access to further workings of the idea.

Politicians are very important in these processes. They are, of course, among the ranks of the early users, and their usage is a crucial *rite de passage* for every phenomenon which is in process of becoming a paradigm. Political usage signals that an idea is passing from theory to metaphor. All the great breakthroughs and fresh paradigms of science evolve into metaphorical material at later stages. The term paradigm is itself an example of what I mean.[5] Indeed, the metaphors remain as historical evidence of scientific turning-points.

Perhaps the most far-reaching and enduring of all is the metaphor of discovery applied to the evolution of science and expressed as its central method. This we derive from Francis Bacon's *Novum Organum*, in which he draws attention to the three great *discoveries* that have exerted more power over the affairs of humankind than any statesman: gunpowder, the magnet and printing. 'For these three have changed the whole face and state of things throughout the world ... in so far that no empire, no sect, no star seems to have exerted greater power and influence in human affairs than these mechanical discoveries.'[6] Bacon sees discovery as the greatest form of human achievement. Power may be sought for 'vulgar and degenerate' motives, when a person wants it for himself; it may be sought for reasons of national covetousness, which is somewhat more noble. But noblest of all motives for seeking power is the aspiration to assist the human race in gaining dominion over the universe. The belief that scientific and technological discoveries are historic achievements in a long quest to dominate nature is perhaps the grandest of all of the images we hold in our minds about science. It is in many ways the opposite of the ecological image, which suggests that humanity is, and ought to be, the subject of nature rather than its aggrandizing monarch.

Now, my real purpose is to explore one massive paradigm that is haunting and influencing the world at the present time. It is the *Novum Organum* of the moment. It has firmly invaded academia, politics, industry and a great range of scientific fields. I am referring to the notion of information – especially as applied in the widespread concept of an 'information revolution' – and its many current derivatives. For centuries, knowledge, news, literature, personal messages have been exchanged by a proliferating variety of methods: paper, printing, canvas, tiles, vinyl, celluloid, ink, paint, 3-D. Only a matter of a few decades ago, it became evident that every form of communication was capable of being reduced to the condition of data, then stored and retransmitted in some suitable medium. We began to realize that it was possible to think about all of these, whether they end up as text, sound or still or moving image, as data or information. We realized that the information contained within, say, a picture can be extracted from the supporting medium and held for posterity, or for rapid onward communication in the form of computer data. Whatever the source of the communication, whatever the ultimate means of delivering the message, the material passed through the condition of being information. The world came to appear constituted of information. Information thus came to provide one of the transforming, paradigmatic ideas of the century.

It is transforming in the sense that, once our minds have made the necessary adjustments, the thought ends in transforming whole areas of public thinking. The political changes that resulted in the collapse of the Communist world system and the end of the Cold War, for example, owed a great deal to the fact that one could now describe all forms of communication as manifestations of this same thing, information. Thus it became absurd for governments to attempt to arrest the circulation of certain types of knowledge about events, when the same data-stream had become the carrier of necessary industrial, economic and technical information. We often, in the 1990s, fail to realize how profound the change has been in the way we envisage the collectivity of the means of knowledge and communication. Moreover, the term itself, once it passed into the political language and more generally into the language of policy, has acted as a spur to whole areas of physical change. Libraries, telephone systems, the organization of the retailing of software, the advent of CD and CD-ROM, all found their path forward into the era of adaptation and retooling cleared for them by the fact that the mental image and the terminology of the 'information revolution' were suddenly available.

The sheer semantic spread the term has achieved owes much to the discovery of DNA, and thus the further adaptation of the idea that information is the organizing principle of life itself, key to explaining the operations of the living cell. Indeed, John Maynard Smith explains how the concept of information applies in modern molecular biology not as metaphor, but as a literal account of the operations of the genetic code. August Weismann discovered a century ago that heredity is about 'the transmission, not of matter or energy, but of information'. The technical terms include messenger, code, transcription, translation, proofreading. The notion of information has entered many of the paradigms that sustain our understanding of the world.[7] At the same time, the image of a macro-information revolution has added fuel to a political movement that encourages all manner of political changes in the direction of privatization and corporate competition. It is difficult to keep track of its rapidly flowing career. It seems to me that, far from nearing the end of its mental trajectory, it has still a good way to go.

Information is in some ways the most typical of the transforming concepts I have in mind, because it has become a powerful banner as well as a powerful metaphor. When French politicians, for example, talk about *informatisation*, it is now hard to tell whether this is policy or observation. When the imagination of people who hold authority is touched, an image becomes more than a flourish, more than a useful way of looking – it acquires a normative, regulatory role. Institutions incorporate the phrase and try to conform to the idea it enshrines.

More than two decades have passed since Daniel Bell and Fritz Machlup wrote books[8] suggesting that the industrial economy was turning into an information economy. Their *grande idée* was that a second – or rather third – industrial revolution was taking place in the mid-twentieth century. The agricultural economy had once acted as the support of the feudal system, but had given way to new classes and a new industrial economy in the late eighteenth century. That industrial revolution – itself a metaphor to explain the absence of a French-style social revolution – passed through several phases,[9] including the grand retooling and reorganization represented by automation after the Second World War. Now a new 'revolution' – by the 1950s the word had lost most of its historical overtones and had come simply to mean 'change' – was taking place that was putting services before manufacturing. For Daniel Bell, the revolution was leading towards a 'post-industrial' society in which services played a much greater role than in previous generations. Later, he noticed the way in which information machinery was becoming attached to an array of manufacturing and extractive processes, so he and many followers adopted the notion that the world was passing into the phase of 'information society'. It was by no means irrelevant that the intellectuals of the West were at that time feeling the need for a substitute for Marxist ideology, which had itself provided a transportable, but now outworn, post-Hegelian tripartite model to describe the supposed patterns in human history.

Fritz Machlup produced the arithmetical data, in studies which led up to his 1980 book *The Production and Distribution of Knowledge in the USA*.[10] This showed that in the course of a century the proportion of American workers engaged in agriculture had fallen from 40 per cent to about 4 per cent, while the proportion of industrial workers was also then beginning to fall. Meanwhile, the proportion of 'information' workers had risen from 4 per cent to 50 per cent. Of course, it is easier now to see how this analysis resulted, at least in part, from juggling with figures and categories. Naturally, all jobs had altered during the course of the previous century, and do constantly alter, in content as well as in the tools they employ. But did the users of the new computers and word-processors and communication devices constitute a new class in any real sense? And was this class a kind of extension of the intelligentsia, in the sense that all its supposed members, from booking clerk to Regius Professor would now recognize one another as fellow knowledge-workers or information colleagues? These possibilities added to the spirit of optimism that surrounded Information Society thinking. The social and political analysis that emanated from the idea of post-industrialism was crucial to its popularity. Post-industrialism attractively suggested a more even distribution of power throughout society. It suggested that a new technical and managerial cohort was becoming the leading occupational group – substituting, in a way, for now-jettisoned notions of a ruling class. The old political debates would fade away and give place to a politics of groups and causes. At the heart of this idea was the belief that the popularization of further education in the 1960s was giving rise to an explosive growth in scientific, research and technical occupations. This growth did not in fact take place as envisaged, and in any case was not socially or organically linked with the spread of information technology-based occupations in the general work-force. Most of these were really, and are really, connected with the administration and facilitation of economic and industrial activities. A shift of the work-force beyond the Western economies was taking place, part of a broader process of globalizing production – a process perhaps still gaining momentum. As the years have passed, the negative aspects of the change have become more evident, particularly the impact on employment within capitalist economies and the impact on the traditional culture of the Third World societies to which much of the humdrum industrial work was being, and is still being, exported.

But today, no election is possible without a promise of progress in the information sphere. The idea has become fused with notions of freedom, the free flow of ideas, and freedom of speech itself. Those metaphorical extensions and flourishes are not wrong or fraudulent, but they do illustrate how a dynamic of change operates in human society, how labels and memorable images conjure policies into programmes, how they reassure, how they furnish the political imperatives.

In March 1994 the Vice-President of the United States delivered a speech to the International Telecommunications Union Conference in Buenos Aires, during which he extended to the international sphere one of his and Mr Clinton's domestic election promises of 1992.[11] He declared that the creation of a Global Information Infrastructure (GII) would 'provide the world with a set of superhighways on which all people can travel'. He was silently, romantically, recalling the role his father had played in working for the real highway system of America in the 1950s, and in his mind the farrago of fibre and satellite links, the construction of which he and the President had decided to encourage, was a metaphorical road network. The visionary promises that flow from the superhighway metaphor are a good example of reductionist policy-making. Mr Gore said: 'We can now at last create a planetary information network that transmits messages and images with the speed of light from the largest city to the smallest village on every continent.'[12] The Vice-President opened up a vista of grand technological solutions to issues of human welfare and the control of societies, weaving his futuristic tapestry with the warp of cliché and the woof of optimistic analogy: 'I see a new Athenian Age of democracy forged in the fora the GII will create.'

Already, he explained, 60 per cent of all US workers are 'knowledge workers', and their swelling numbers would drive the global economy towards hundreds of billions of dollars worth of economic growth. Now you might, encouraged by the Vice-President, hope to become a 'knowledge worker', but when you are appointed your task may still be selling subway tickets to commuters or organizing the files of a stockbroker. And yet what he said was not at all wrong, but merely hopeful in a special political way (when we say today that someone is a good communicator, that is often what we mean). The aura of knowing triumphalism that is made to surround the information idea tends to neglect the continuities, the realization that there are many things that do not change, and others that change in unforeseen or unacceptable ways. It is the language chosen that hurries the cause onwards, excluding other inexpressible paths and making an obviousness of its own visibility. It is what the writers of the Bible would have recognized instantly as idolatry. Fresh visions turn into words, words which seem to have meaning and therefore power.

The idea that we were moving into an 'information society', and that now indeed we live in one, implied that this was a society in which the majority of people had come to spend their time carrying out tasks connected with information – collecting and expressing it, storing, retrieving and disseminating it. There were no information revolutionaries, but instead a number of people attempting to generalize upon a number of noted but previously unconnected statistical trends. In particular, the changing labour market appeared to confirm the notion that a fundamental change was occurring in the disposition of working time. There were military as well as commercial and governmental factors pushing the whole thing forwards – not least because of the need to standardize certain forms of equipment and various ways of transmitting information through wire and ether. But there was no party for revolution, there was no overwhelming necessity, no dominating factor, only a number of institutions that saw in the marriage of computing with telecommunications a way to economize in the use of expensive resources.

Solid-state electronics could have evolved along quite different technical paths – it passed through many byways of technological change and was shaped by social as well as logical or scientific factors.

The prophecies had more of a Hegelian ring about them. Information technology was penetrated by the historic spirit. It was or is the third age of the economic world, after the agricultural and industrial eras. Knowledge, expertise and information were to become the main variables, replacing labour and capital in the modern economy.

The very act of formulating this idea of an information and communication society has exercised much of the transforming power, or has at least provided the political acceleration. It is the label that encouraged educators to seize upon information equipment and use it to alter curricula, and by so doing to encourage children to believe that the computer somehow captures the essence of the working of the human mind. It was the label also that captivated official and party think-tanks. In France, Simon Nora and Alain Minc,[13] in a report that in the 1970s helped launch the quest for a national *télématique*, revealed the political dynamic of the term itself and of its cognate expression, *informatisation*. In France, the process of constructing an information society did not, as in the USA and the UK, fit doctrinally with a political insistence on the primacy of private capital in laying down the new infrastructures. In the 1980s, country after country produced national plans that used the term 'information society' as the key. Japan was the first to do so, but Canada, Australia, the UK, France and Germany followed within months or years. All of them hammered home the belief that information machines would produce a new kind of society.

Yonedji Masuda, for example, described the coming 'computopia' as 'a society that brings about a general flourishing state of human intellectual creativity, instead of affluent material consumption'.[14] Japan built new suburbs and one wholly new town[15] swathed in new communications technology as an optimistic experiment in this new kind of society. In the new town, every kitchen in every house was equipped with a special television camera that could communicate with all the other homes in the town. The content proved to be somewhat limited.

The dystopian critique both of the computer as a human tool and of the whole idea of a 'third wave' of capitalist society was well established before the giant process of retooling the Western economy got under way. Jacques Ellul, in a prescient warning against the encircling power of *technique*, suggested that the modern world was investing all technology, or *technicisme*, with the quality of the sacred. Ellul wrote *The Technological Society*[16] in the 1950s, but at a moment when computers and systems analysis were already topics of discussion, and it did much to establish the idea of technology as sentient, animistic, autonomous. And he saw *technique* as the central *enjeu* or gambler's stake of the twentieth century, rather than as a response to needs, a set of attempted solutions to its problems. More frequent have been the anxieties that the computer would become a Frankenstein, taking from civilization its control over its own processes, rather than civilization using the machine, belatedly, to regain such control from the processes of industrialization. Theodore Roszak, for example, warns against the effects of educators' enthusiasm for inculcating the increasingly fashionable 'computer literacy'. He writes about the 'treacherous deception ... that exercises in programming and game playing are somehow giving them control over a powerful technology'.[17] Ellul wrote his book in the late 1950s, Roszak in the 1980s.

The objections of Michael Shallis, writing in 1984, are that human beings are being forced into a false self-definition, that increasing reliance upon the computer is becoming a form of idolatry. The human race was equipping itself with a mechanized rationality that was, to use the title of his book, a 'silicon idol'.[18] But the Utopian visions exceeded the dystopian by a large factor: *Silicon Civilization*, *The Wired Society*, *The Mighty Micro*, *Technologies of Freedom* and their companions have greatly outnumbered such titles as *Electronic Illusions* and *Electronic Nightmare*.

If you work your way through this literature, you begin to detect an undertow, an unexplicit, almost subterfuge train of thought that emanates from the late Cold War context. During the seemingly unending era of the Cold War (which when it ended, did so quite suddenly), there was the need to maintain a set of substitute discourses for the grand narrative of Marxism. There was also a feeling that the hopes of the 1960s had never reached a resolution, a confirmation of the media visions and technological improvisations with which that generation had been saturated. The 1960s and 1970s vision of the computer were often seen by people who were seeking a firm basis for a renewed humanistic optimism. At its most simplistic, the information society was something to look forward to, a case of renewable History. For many it still is.

But it must have been a mistake to build a futuristic vision around a single technology. The first and second industrial revolutions had had one dominating technology – the steam engine – and thus it was easy to leap to an assertion that the computer would perform the same role during Alvin Toffler's 'Third Wave'. There was a degree of straightforward technological determinism in this analysis, but also a failure to look at all the other strands of history that would play their part, particularly those economic processes that are not technological in nature. The growing prosperity associated with the computerization of production, together with the rapid growth in the means of entertainment, means there is a larger class of young people with time to spend on the arts – both traditional and innovative forms. But throughout the new global economy there have also been processes of a distinctly dystopian kind at work: vast numbers of refugees, a large swathe of uneducated youth, homeless, jobless, their lives lacking any form of moral outlook, an apparently unreachable army of urban homeless, and a new criminal class able to use the new technology in pursuit of money for drugs, unearned luxury or mere survival. So widespread and so intractable and so widespread have been the dysfunctions that they tend sometimes to obscure the optimism that was the essence of the post-Hippie information society idea.

Mr Gore's information superhighway, enmeshed with the superhighways of a hundred other nations, will multiply access to myriad forms of information for billions of people. There is the same open-hearted innocence about it. Censorship of information and the control of minds will become impossible. Markets of data will form within markets of networks, and through the trial and error of the market some sort of rational assembly of communication systems will emerge. But many traditional distinctions are being eroded, notably those between mass and personal forms of communication. The mass media of cinema, newspapers and television will, of course, continue to exist, and indeed new opportunities will open up for them. The advanced electronic media – databases, multimedia computers – that have so far remained somewhat specialized, confined within a group of *aficionados*, are pushing at these boundaries, attempting to adapt to the desires of the mass consumer; in other words, they are trying to find entertainment services that millions of people will buy.

Then there is a wholly new range of personal electronic media: networks that evade all the commercial entertainment and information systems and are rooted in the aspirations of a new class of enthusiasts. Internet is a high-speed linkage of ten thousand databases that now has anything up to 35 million US and other users. It belongs in the family of amateur communications, like Citizen Band radio, facsimile or the private newsletter. It crosses the boundaries between the person-to-person telephonic mode and small-group communications, and appears to have established a breakthrough into viability beyond the academic groups that were its pioneers. But already, the sheer quantity and range of information that can be explored, exchanged or distributed through Internet suggest a formation new in the history of human discourse. The micro-social model for it is the seminar. The system makes room for personal initiative in originating and exchanging information within an electronic medium. Around Internet, it is possible to re-evoke the optimistic, democratizing, socially cohering predictions that surrounded the 'information society' idea a decade ago. But the system, as it has grown, presents a regulatory challenge, for the sheer attractiveness of its lack of regulation means that it is open to many forms of manipulation and unsupervised commercial hucksterism. Yet to regulate it would inevitably be to sequestrate what custom and practice have now established as an open right to an open medium. Only the push and pull of economic and political interests will resolve the ultimate shape of this new medium, as well as that of at least a dozen other innovative technologies and services.

It is possible that a new generation will turn to computers for information, rather than to mass media. The market tests the validity of aspirations within the information profusion; but alas, there are no flat playing fields on which the many-sided dialogue can occur, only the bumpy terrain left behind by previous contestants.

The interventions of the Clinton administration will cause a fresh wave of turbulence within a vast and growing industry, and facilitate great changes in shopping, entertainment and education. The governmental message is simultaneously ideological, economic, industrial and political. It indicates that it has espoused a cause, one which permits it to adopt a visionary stance, to readjust itself in the public imagination. The National and Global Information Infrastructures are paths that disappear into a mist, with a major junction ahead. One way leads via Internet, or some adaptation of it, to an information culture based upon the abundant supply and rapid transmission of large quantities of material, visual, textual, aural, or all of these in combination. Another possible route, favoured at one time by British governments, was that of an entertainment-led evolution sometimes labelled the Superhighway –a term that is being widely used without either precision or general agreement as to its meaning. Both paths, it is believed, will end beyond the clouds at the same ultimate destination: the society of information abundance, freely available in mass, person-to-person and 'seminar' modes.

In other words, two forces have identified themselves in the fray: one a spontaneous demand for a grand amassing of all forms of communication and information into a kind of latter-day Alexandrian Library, which may or may not ultimately find an economic role for itself; the other emanates from traditional mass-media entertainment interests. Only ideology leads, beyond the horizon, beyond the imaginable outcome of imaginable markets, to a common destination, the totally interactive information society.

The rise of the information economy has revealed the centrality of information processing and communication to the workings of human society. If you look at all the defining properties of living things, from homeostasis to metabolic growth, all the processes that constitute adaptation (conditioning, imprinting, learning) and reproduction, you find that they can all be made explicable and mutually consistent by imagining them as systems of information, ways of circulating instructions. Without this reductionist metaphorical application of the idea of information, it would be difficult to explain, to reveal, the working of the DNA molecule.

But has there been an underlying galvanic force making information necessary as a contemporary paradigm? It would appear so. Information crises became endemic within the capitalist system from the middle of the last century. For example, keeping track of freight wagons in the massive US railroad system brought in its wake problems of managerial control – what we would call problems of information processing – that would have prevented further growth had not separate systems for handling the information itself evolved. Managing the handling of containers within a shipping operation, booking tickets for planes, ships and trains, running the timetabling of transportation systems, manufacturing the spare parts for mass consumer goods ranging from pianos to motor cars: all gradually became, or would have become, impossible without paratechnologies for collating the information. The work-force necessary to carry out this task itself became burdensome to the industrial processes it was meant to facilitate.

The computer generation of text was itself the result of a quest to automate the physical hot-lead processes entailed in traditional printing, the oldest of all the industrial technologies. Paper money had been an early example of the attempt to transmute a physical substance, coinage, into the information mode. The postage stamp was a special subdivision of paper money. The motion picture transmuted and industrialized the medium of theatre, film being another way of registering and replicating a physical activity. The idea of automating information itself had thus been creeping up on capitalist society for over a century, as a way of mending the many dislocations and managerial nightmares resulting from spiralling production capacity. In his book *The Control Revolution*,[19] James Beniger tries to demonstrate the smoothness of the transition to the microprocessor; and seen in long-shot, as it were, the computerization of text does look like a simple continuation of a long series of attempts to regain control over human processes that were advancing too rapidly for their own easy management.

The process had been gathering pace since the first mature stage of the industrial system, in the 1840s, and it moved from one line of technological history to another, one form of energy to another, until the advent of the microprocessor. What we are witnessing in the 1990s is the growing transparency of the information machinery, and its spreading through society to non-specialist communities. With 35 million users of Internet, the breakthrough has perhaps already occurred to a society in which information exchange is ready to be more fully interactive, in which physical distance has finally ceased to be a factor in the cost of transporting information, in which the disparity between individual communication and audience communication appears to be coming to an end.

With the fixing of those principles, with the sheer multiplicity of content and universality of the nodes of the resulting network, we are looking at a necessary reshaping of our image of what a society is. The cascading of messages is analogous to what occurs in the activation of a neural network, when cells 'emerge' at the point where the activity achieves a self-consistent state. It is helpful to apply the image of 'emergence' to the phenomenon of a totally interactive and abundant system of social information. For this may now be in the process of formation. When such a phenomenon reaches its own mature level, a fresh phenomenon should spontaneously occur. No one can say at what level of installation and exploitation of new communication devices this state of 'emergence' will arrive. But it will have to be a *cultural* state, a condition that historians will later see as a turning-point towards a new way of life. The phenomenon of emergence is a way of looking at historical processes as if they are processes of nature. The making of prophecies is a necessary part of the process, even though the results always lie beyond the skills of prophecy or extrapolation.

If you imagine all the atoms in a pan of water as they react to the application of heat, you see a steady process taking place, hardly altering until moments before boiling point is reached, when the atoms suddenly move to a peak of excitement: then very quickly they are transformed into steam.[20] If you plot the line of human history – or just the history of systems of human communication – against the historical pattern of the boiling pan of water, you can see how long the slow build-up takes, and how quickly the emergence phenomenon occurs when it arrives. Once the new 'state' is formulated, everything previous to it rapidly acquires the sepia tone of distant history. It is rather like trying to remember, after the arrival of Yeltsin, what the reign of Brezhnev was like. Something was changing very slowly in a society of infinite frustrations, until the sheer accumulation of those frustrations brought about a change in historical conditions that turned out to be qualitative rather than quantitative. From inside the society it was hard to see how great or how sudden the change would be.

One can draw parallels with the sudden arrival of printing after decades of evolution in the numbers of users and creators of text, until the point when technological possibilities, markets, creative ideas and cultural needs suddenly converged. Printing spread throughout the world in a decade. Western economies have been slowly building up towards a change since the new information systems began developing, one by one, using many different technologies, starting many decades ago.

A society seldom recognizes itself on rereading the predictions from which it sprang. The facts that time ultimately exposes are expressed in prose, but the promises were in poetry. Politics lives as it were in the subjunctive, while government can only speak in the indicative; what fills the expressive gap between the ways we envisage the future and the ways the future behaves in its turn, arises from a mysterious interaction between change and the recurring images of change.

FIVE

New Technologies and New Illusions

We have begun to give up seeing this century as a series of culminations. The twentieth century's extraordinary involvements with technology, art, warfare and medicine are now, at the century's end, felt to be mere moments in much longer processes, rather than a series of (usually devastating) fulfilments. This fact – or feeling – is one of the more beneficial aspects of what Fredric Jameson calls the 'inverted millenarianism'[1] of the late twentieth century: the practice of naming books the 'End' of something, and renaming familiar phenomena by inserting the prefix 'Post'. The media of cinema and television between them played a great part in creating the sense of culmination in respect of the century's cultural apparatus. They are in themselves good examples of the way twentieth-century things have arrogated to themselves the claim to be fulfilling some long-standing aspiration.

Cinema, when its various lines of technical evolution came together at the turn of the century, advertised itself as a kind of ultimate solution to the inadequacies of earlier methods of representation. Today we can see that cinema has only been the beginning of something, and by inverting its attendant millenarianism, we can perhaps begin to see how it achieved its earlier captivation. Our conventions of perception, the prevailing sensorium of the West, were captured by one particular means, a specific industry of culture, and now, released from it, we are available for fresh forms of experience, new illusory pleasures. Cinema and television dominated our ways of representing the world. Now, as they themselves pass into history, their off-spring technologies suggest different ways of representing that world.

When Baudelaire saw the obsessive interest generated by the new photographic technologies of the 1850s, his reaction took the form of an antiquarian scorn: 'Those thousands of hungry eyes ... bending over the peepholes of the stereoscope, as though they were the attic-windows of the infinite.'[2] Today, we too are present at the opening stages of a new generation of technologies that promise in some sense to refresh our habits of perception; virtual reality, for example, may be offering us a similar chance either to be scornful or to give indulgent encouragement. Virtual Reality and High Definition Television are not yet media, and their arrival as familiar, transparent technologies, if it occurs, will be part of that now-emergent state of information culture discussed in the last chapter, not yet possible to discern. But they have advanced sufficiently for cinema and television to begin to look antique, to diminish in first-order enthralment, to reveal their cumbersomeness.

In the making of representations, whether in writing, sound or image, this century has sought to fulfil an ancient quest, the progressive search for perfect descriptions of the world, for exactitude of representation. The establishment of the medium of cinema had a kind of 'at last!' about it. André Bazin, whose voice dominated the discussion of cinema for two decades, thought, like the Victorians before him, that the whole purpose of photography was to recreate, to 'embalm', a perfect illusion of the world of perception. The *ambition* of cinematography was to reproduce the real. As Bazin wrote:

[86]

The objective nature of photography confers on it a quality of credibility absent from all other picture-making ... A very faithful drawing may actually tell us more about the model but despite the promptings of our critical intelligence it will never have the irrational power of the photograph to bear away our faith ... for photography does not create eternity, as art does, it embalms time, rescuing it simply from its proper corruption.[3]

The ultimate aspiration was the achievement, through constant refinement of the available technical means, of what Bazin called Total Cinema.

Even in the earliest days of cinema, its practitioners were aware of the difficulty of drawing a line between the obvious reproductive, mirroring functions of the camera and its potential for enhancing its images by 'unnatural' means. Dziga Vertov (1896–1954), a Russian who came to be regarded as the Ur-Father of the English documentary movement, explored while at Petrograd in 1916 the camera's potential to illuminate life 'as it is', and saw how the camera can do something more than the human eye.[4] He noted 'the utilization of the camera as a cinema eye for the purpose of research into the chaos of visual phenomena filling the universe'. The camera *researched into* vision, and was a tool that illuminated reality as much as it reflected it. But all the other tools of exact representation share this characteristic; they all supply, through the exaggerating capacity of their particular natures, a singular vision. Whether based upon speech, handwriting, printing, sound recording or photography, each medium has emphasized a different sense and transmuted its message in accordance with the needs of a human sense or a piece of equipment that relates to one of the senses. Change in the culture of communication, as Donald Lowe puts it, 'ultimately leads to change in the hierarchy of sensing'.[5] But the human senses do appear to be biased towards positivism; there seems to be a built-in alertness of the sensorium to images that reproduce the world. Susan Sontag might say this was a latent desire for possession, for turning the world, by means of camera or recorder, into property.[6] One of the sensed 'culminations' of twentieth-century moving-image media was that labelled by Donald Lowe and others as the 'bourgeois mode of representation', a way of seeing that ends in possessing, and which appeared to many, especially those writing during the 1960s, as an ultimate and ineluctable mode of perception.

The invention of Pitman's shorthand in the early nineteenth-century world of newspaper reporting had generated a comparable set of expectations; shorthand also is a way of taking possession of perceived phenomena and transporting them through society.[7] For the first time, it was possible to acquire, after brief training, the skill of reproducing a speaker's *ipsissima verba*. Until then, a mere impression had been the best that could be provided, even though there had long been private forms of shorthand; there had also been individuals like 'Memory' Woodfall, who in the 1760s claimed that, because of his special mental powers, he could recall Parliamentary speeches *verbatim* and regurgitate them an hour later to suit the needs of the printing house. But these were stunts, and a great deal of the resulting material was concocted. Charles Dickens was one of the new breed of stenographer-reporters of the 1830s, armed with the new skill of shorthand through which the true dimensions of reality could be flawlessly recovered, the speed of the impact enhanced by the device of the electric telegraph. 'Telegrams are for facts,' ordered a thrifty managing director of *The Times* later in the century. 'Opinion and comment can come by post.'[8]

But reality cannot be reconstructed or reconstituted out of

words or facts alone, if at all. Parliament and the courts of law clung to, lived by, pure verbal reproduction, but the quest for realistic reproduction of statements has continued until our own day, with new and uncertain experiments in videoed evidence. The arrival of photography marked a new and important stage in the attempt to arrest reality, to preserve events for cultural, political, bureaucratic purposes.

In the early nineteenth century, photography appeared to offer irrefutable proof of the existence of an objective world. Indeed, the project is older than photography or shorthand; its inspiration is in Bacon and Descartes. Between Galileo and Newton, there existed an encouragingly regular world in which everything could be observed, measured and increasingly laid open to proof through experiment. The era of the Renaissance delighted in lenses, astronomic telescopes, visual prostheses of many kinds. The reality of objects consisted in the information that emanated from them and entered our consciousness. All the sciences of description – botany, zoology, anatomy, palaeontology, astronomy, physics – had a profound yearning, a need for the amenity which photography conferred.[9]

Einstein pointed to the contradiction inherent in this accepted view of reality when he revealed that time and space were also concepts within our consciousness, like other predispositions of perception that gave us our sense of the world's objective reality. But cinema and television have until the present moment continued to live with, and within, a Cartesian cosmos. Every new addition to the armoury of technique, from fast film-stock and miniature tape to the long-distance lens, was harnessed to the project of achieving a more exact representation of the real.

In painting and architecture, the great project of Western perception finds expression, for example, in Renaissance experiments with perspective. Donatello's exploration of *rilievo*, the use of deep and shallow relief, extended the repertory of perspective into a new medium, and perhaps provided its audience with the sensation, one familiar to us, of being present at a revelation, a new era in reproduced realism.[10] The Donatello experience might have been not unlike that provided by the first 3-D films in the 1950s: *Bwana Devil* of 1953 was advertised with the promise of 'A lion in your lap, a lover in your arms!'[11] This great project of realism was the quest of centuries; its line of descent is different from that of other kinds of art. It sought out the senses of touch, sight and hearing. It passed through children's toys, fairground displays, the daguerreotype, the phenakistiscope, even the barrel-organ. Auerbach pursues it through the world of letters.[12] The novel is a perspectival experiment in typographic space as much as a painting by Leonardo is in visual space. Both are attempts at gratifying a profound emotional and cultural need to hold reality in a state of captivity, to seize a second chance of experience; an opportunity to reach beyond normal physical capability, to continue receiving the pleasure a child experiences in opening a box of perfect miniature lead soldiers, or a reader entering the illusionistic narrative space of a Trollope novel. 'With this drop of ink at the end of my pen, I will show you the roomy workshop of Jonathan Burge, carpenter and builder in the village of Hayslope, as it appeared on the 18th June, in the year of our Lord, 1799.' Thus George Eliot opens her novel *Adam Bede*. The writing becomes a tool of reproductive demonstration. We are being made, as Ortega y Gasset put it, to enjoy a novel by being surrounded by it on all sides. The hypnotic illusionism of the novel is denounced today by those who want to unmask the genre, and indeed other narrative realist genres, for its covert ideological domination, because its trick of verisimilitude is (in the accusing phrases of Walter Benjamin) an aesthetically inauthentic, oneiric Freudian wish-fulfilment.[13]

But let us return to the moving image, and focus our attention on the implications of some of the newest ways of securing and communicating images and sounds. The Victorian search for a means of creating the illusion of photographic movement was a long drawn-out affair that came to a kind of climax in the 1890s. Marey had established the phenomenon we know as persistence of vision, the inability of the human eye to register as separate entities a flow of images occurring at more than a certain speed. All the Victorian devices (including television) exploit this phenomenon in one way or another, whether in a flip-book or a zoetrope.[14] There were in fact two different but overlapping historical strands, the former attempting to reproduce 'reality' in order to analyse and explain it, the latter attempting to exploit the same perceptual phenomenon (persistence of vision) to produce fantasy and illusion, to create, from the human imaginative repertory, a simulated world – and make it move.

The former, scientific line of development was concerned with taking the work of the laboratory into the real world, and bothered little about the potential of the resulting devices to reproduce as illusions the ways of the living world; the latter was an outright illusionistic quest in which the inventors permitted their devices to be taken into the fairground, to be manufactured as expensive toys. Eadweard Muybridge's project was to study animal locomotion, and there survive his sequences of photographs of a naked man rowing, and of horses and other animals in motion, that aimed, by breaking down the event into a series of still frames, to describe and illuminate scientifically the workings of the real world normally inaccessible to human vision;[15] the Lumière brothers placed their camera in front of episodes of ordinary life in order to fascinate their audiences with a naturalistic replica. Then Méliès, the father of cinematic fantasy, introduced a world of enthralling inventions, essentially animated cartoons fixed on strips of celluloid. These different lines of exploitation reflected different ideological drives and possessed different cultural implications.

Within a few decades the artist Len Lye – and many others – were using the cinematographic image in a non-photographic mode, sometimes drawing direct rather than photographing their animated figures on frames of film.[16] The cinema exploited a fundamental divergence that had been present in all art-forms, one strand based upon ever more precise and convincing realism, the other consisting of animated distortions, tricks and illusions derived from the fairground and the fairy tale – a tradition as ancient as cave-paintings but, in its essence, external to the great realist project.

One Athanasius Kirch in 1640 wrote a treatise on *The Great Art of Light and Shadows*, but seems neither to have experimented nor to have constructed a device. But in his diary for 1666 Samuel Pepys reports going to a house where 'a lanthorn with pictures in glass' threw images on a wall. Huyghens had already described the Lanterna Magica in the 1650s. A century later, France saw the magic lantern into a new age with the Phantasmagoria, a macabre post-Revolutionary entertainment in which audiences were thrilled by groans and shrieks, claps of thunder and the howling of wind. Benjamin Franklin suggested a way to enhance the efforts with his glass harmonica. The moving image was, it appears, a tool of the Gothic temperament.

The moving image in its cinematic guise emerged from a fusion of the two strands of technical evolution, at a point of conjunction between a theatrical tradition that yearned for verisimilitude – a technical search for ways of recording, reproducing, 'conserving' the experience of the world (telephone, phonograph, camera) – and the cultural desire of late romanticism to achieve intense enthralment, a by-passing of the intellect in the attempt to seize the emotions.

Well before the middle of the nineteenth century, audiences had grown used to dramatic visual effects at the Panorama and Diorama shows, which exploited all the new sources of illumination (limelight, gas, electricity). Enormous halls were filled with double, triple and quadruple images; images produced by slides were made to move cinematically, as it were. In one venue, the audience was seated in simulated railway carriages while two vast illuminated panoramas were pulled at left and right to create simulated landscapes. Cinema thus continued and enhanced an already established visual tradition, and the perceptual faculties of audiences were already trained to 'frame' the moving image before Edison, the Lumières and Méliès came on the scene.[17]

We sometimes forget the sheer number of technologies that have been developed in our own times to present enhanced moving images, ever more enthralling and in the realist tradition. There were several attempts in the post-war era at three-dimensional cinema. There was Todd-AO and then the various other forms of wide-screen vision, until the specialist vast-screen media of IMAX and Omnimax arrived. Film stock was used in 70 mm width to create an ever more perfect image. There was Cinemascope and Cinerama, with three cameras lashed together creating the images to feed three corresponding cinema projectors that threw their images on to a vast concave screen. Much twentieth-century technology simply returns to more ancient systems: magic-lantern shows of the 1890s also used triple images and vast screens. And so did Abel Gance in 1927 in parts of *Napoleon*. Similar multi-form images had been demonstrated at the Paris World Exposition of 1900.

Of course, the demarcation between the quest for realism and the quest for illusion is not total and not without exceptions or complications. Realism in moving pictures, or in any other form of representation, is only a more convincing way of achieving an illusion. Every fresh device brought to the task of making moving images renders them more deeply convincing, but at the same time renders inadequate the earlier devices that until then had provided a satisfyingly complete experience (or illusion). Our sensorium responds to training or conditioning, and comes to feel deceived or let down when a better mode of illusion, laying claim to being a culminating mode, turns up. The repeat of a 1960s television programme possesses a quaintness, even if we saw it when it was new. To look at newsreels from the First World War is like staring at old manuscripts. What we bring to the act of looking is our hungry visual ambition, our restless urge to refine our individual role within the working Western sensorium.

The case of the compact disc is instructive. It has rapidly outstripped earlier forms of commercial recording because it provides a more perfect, less 'artificial', sound. It gives the illusion of a total rendition of the music, as if our perspective were at the centre of the sound. But this is a special kind of illusion produced through digitization. A digital medium – whether it provides text, moving image or merely sound – reduces an event to numbers, embeds them in a memory or a physical substance from which a systematic regeneration of the original event is possible. A digital recording is the transcription of a series of symbols; an analogue recording is a tracing of an actual event. To play back from an analogue recording is rather like stripping a photographic print from a negative. It is an imprint of reality, the mark made by an original event. The digital medium is a transported illusion – offering greater verisimilitude – of a real experience.[18]

Throughout history, the sensorium has been trained to

respond to systems of communication and of art that are essentially analogues. Our institutions of education, art and politics are among the organizational consequences of these same systems of perception. Our culture celebrates a world of objects. We take care to prevent paintings being damaged, even by the glancing touch of an admiring viewer. We mount elaborate guard over collections of books and manuscripts. When we take a photograph, we may be obsessively anxious to prevent any interference with the lens, or with the negative of the resulting print. Every scratch or smudge is a disaster.

Progressive degradation of the original – whether oil painting, lithograph or videotape – is the inevitable and irreversible consequence of making copies. For there is a finite limit to the reproductive possibilities of any medium created in analogue mode. Indeed, originals using any available form of physical base inevitably become the objects of a kind of cult, usually but not always expressed in commercial terms.

But the digital mode is entirely free of such corruption. It exists as a series of numbers awaiting the summons to the world of human perception, or *interface*. Its blemishes can be removed. It can be limitlessly copied, as it were, or rather, summoned up again to create new copies of itself. A series of numbers is the only 'original', and the series can be repeated without limit, re-expressed, reinterpreted. If you look at the figure on a grocery bill, you hold it as a piece of information in your memory for a moment and inscribe it again on a cheque. A sum – precisely the same sum – is thus transferred from one place to another. The numbers which constitute the digitized version of an opera are transferred simply as information to drive a further device to produce certain effects. The process is quite unlike that of copying a master-tape recording, or impressing paper with an etched plate, or peeling an impression from a cast. The digitizing of objects of perception is a new mode, one already widely practised in our culture, but whose implications are only now beginning to become apparent. Digitization as we know it has been our mental preparation for a more thoroughgoing transmutation of modes, one which must alter the evaluation of forms and objects.[19]

You may recall one of the great debates of the 1980s, the one that raged around the conception of artificial intelligence. The sceptics – John Searle's Reith Lectures were an effective example[20] – argued that a simulation of something was not the same thing as its reality. Artificial intelligence is a machine simulation of what the mind does, like actors in a news bulletin re-enacting a crime; that was not, in Searle's argument, the same as the artificial creation of human intelligence, which could only exist as the activity of a human being. Algorithms cannot constitute consciousness. In the full digitization of sound and image in ordinary domestic devices – something that is now imminent – we are again looking at a means of simulating, creating the complete and satisfying illusion of the act of objective representation. Realism is an activity that lies within the repertoire of digital technology.

One might express this in a different way and say that successful realism on the part of digital technology is a by-product of successful illusionism. Sound and image are now gradually releasing themselves from the physical harness of tape or celluloid strip. They enter computer storage in digitized form and there they are held, reorganized, remade, enhanced, distorted and presented again on demand. The familiar artisanal stability of video and film is collapsing.

Moreover, the digitized image requires no inspiring or originating reality. The *synthesizing* of the real is a paradoxical recursion in media and representational history. It opens up as wide a vista of new creative activity as the coming of cinema. It breaks with photography, and ultimately with cinematography. The illusion created by silent cinema of the train rushing directly at the audience was, at that historical moment, a completely effective perceptual illusion. It would not be so today. But in the birth of Virtual Reality, again as the modern counterpart of a fairground toy, we do have a medium that is similarly enthralling, not yet actualized, institutionalized, encrypted into a medium (to use Seamus Heaney's phrase), but demonstrating a suggestive potential for perfect illusion.

Digital images have already been used to perform feats of illusion that were previously inconceivable, although these tricks and special effects should not conceal from us the greater long-term cultural potential. A deceased popular film star can be revived digitally and made to seem to be speaking lines and acting in a new film. Digitized images can be made to perform actions absent in reality. Simulated people can be snatched out of cyberspace, wholly artificial events can be digitized into wholly convincing ones, convincing in the sense of corresponding in all essentials to the requirements of our sensorium. We would see and hear them as realistically as we see or hear all other events – apart from those at which we are physically present. We see them in a mode indistinguishable from that in which we are accustomed to accepting the records of objective reality. A digitized event can pass every test of verisimilitude. The dinosaurs can materialize – digitally – without recourse to primary genetic material. What we have not yet achieved is the assimilation of this mode into our imaginative apparatus, into the dominant mental machinery of perception.[21]

The video game, the present generation of CD-ROMs and home video are newly created media. Virtual reality is a still-envisaged medium, imagined in science fiction, predicted at conferences, implemented only in hardly satisfying and inchoate forms. A technology turns into a medium in circumstances that depend upon the movements of markets, the recognition of potential social uses, the establishment of perceptual attractiveness.

There are in fact two separate but overlapping processes at work in the present round of transformations: virtuality and interactivity. The popular conception of virtual reality is of a device that provides an intensely heightened realism in which touch, distance, perspective, are adjusted to the will and senses of the individual viewer, to give him or her the sense of being present at an event, rather than merely the viewer of a screen.

All the products so far spun by virtual reality emphasize in their promotion the word 'reality'. The data-gloves and visors connect the viewer to an extremely large processing capacity and insert him or her into a realm of computer-generated images and sounds contrived to represent the entered space as judged from the viewer's presumed perspective. One must also conjecture a video image enhanced to a much greater precision than that with which we are familiar, because of the added possibilities of high definition and high resolution of the image. That is to say, the image will consist of a far greater density of pixels, of moving dots of light, than the best commercial television screen of today.

The subject becomes, as it were, the camera as well as the camera-operator, and is presented with the illusion of scenes that constantly change according to his or her position. Movements of the head, eyes and body control computers that cause this unceasing stream of adjustments. Loose objects have also been taken into the digitized image-store and registered in respect of their position and physical characteristics (colour, shape, surface). But the viewer remains separated from the viewed world and feels a sense of *intense illusion*.

The horizons of the device are strictly perspectival. Virtual reality occurs in Cartesian space. There are currently experiments with force feedback devices that give a sensation of weight and pressure, but these, we are informed, as yet fall short of a directly haptic effect.

The medium is often written about as if it offered an oneiric, absent experience, a substitute for the kind of drugs said to give a sensation of having dreamily opted out of the world. In practice, however, the entire technology is founded upon a reassertion of all the measurable spatial characteristics of the real.[22] It has been described as suggesting to the subject a kind of obsolescence of the body while reproducing illusorily the characteristic movements of one's head and arms.

It is sometimes difficult to see through the over-excited speculation surrounding virtual reality and perceive its own reality – indeed, the belief that virtual reality is an instrument for transforming the self is a crucial element in the cultic aura of the medium as it passes through its pre-natal era. In virtual reality, the human mind and the computer form a kind of alliance to process information in collaboration. Virtual reality is an extension of the imagination as an esemplastic power, as Coleridge might have described it. Imagination is a universal potency in human beings, and virtual reality is its artificial extension, in the sense that a hammer is an extension of the hand and a pocket calculator an extension of the brain.

What virtual reality achieves is the illusion of an immediately responsive environment; it ensures that this environment alters according to the viewer's movement and gesture, and suggests that senses other than eye and ear may one day be made to contribute to the convincingness, enthralment and sensed objectivity of the representation of reality. The principle of virtual reality has, in its simpler forms, a practical potential for helping to reveal the invisible, conjure up the unseeable. A pilot can be trained in a simulated responsive environment in which potential hazards are experienced in virtual form, and in which the artificial environment feeds back the results of his judgements and reactions to situations. An architect can see an imaginary building in three-dimensional form and in its context, and can enter it, furnish it, take it to pieces and reassemble it.

The second principle at work, that of interactivity, is of course increasingly familiar to us in both simple and complex forms. Virtual reality is profoundly interactive in that it responds to the individual viewer's own movements and verbal commands. But given the considerable processing power necessary to establish the medium – vast by the standards of current domestic technologies – one may envisage the additional linkage to large quantities of stored material, to whole visual archives.

One theoretical possibility is that virtual reality might initiate a new form of visual poetry, in which the subject can create and manipulate imagery at will, in illusory three-dimensional space but in real time, drawing from a vast store of digitized images. Interactivity need not be limited, as it is in current experiments, merely to allowing the viewer the possibility of making a series of interventions, such as altering the plot-lines of a drama, or ordering goods from a video catalogue or store, or searching a scientific database, or operating a 'video-by-demand' service. Those represent merely the borderlands of interactivity. The potential exists for the imaginative exploitation of convincing illusions, one that further and more intensely reverses the historic quest for the machinery to represent objective reality.

Something one might describe as a casualty of new media technology is the audience's sense of the legitimacy of images. Earlier twentieth-century history has acquainted us with the airbrush, that simple but necessary tool for making totalitarian history and designing advertisements. The airbrush has separated revolutionary leaders from the history of their revolutions, has helped liquidate opponents of a regime; in the hands of the advertising executive, it can elongate a limb, improve a body-line, straighten a nose. But the digitized image can be altered and manipulated limitlessly and almost instantly. And the virtual reality image, even if it remains but a stunt, goes a giant step further, towards the rearrangement of the possibilities of the sensorium. That long yearned-for sensation of being presented with a perfect representation of the real is in the process of being subverted: the fantasy mode is sequestering the realist mode.

Television audiences are already addicted consumers of images, and have become ever more sophisticated in reading and decoding them. Early cinema audiences learned the grammar of filmic narrative, their minds rapidly attuning to the conventions of cinematic space. Characters in dialogue would appear in neatly reversed angles, movement from left to right of the screen would carry different narrative implications from movement from right to left. With the passage of the years, these were gradually accepted and then exposed as conventions, and the makers of images began deliberately to abandon them. Almost unconsciously, audiences learned to accept the subtle ways cinema and television signalled the difference between genres, and also between sequences of truth and those sequences of fiction. News and documentary always bore a certain style, with natural, unrehearsed sound in the background, with that grainy look that separated news from fictional narrative. But technology at the end of the century reduces these characteristics to mere reading conventions. The variable legitimacies of the moving image are all being challenged. The technological exigencies of the signalling systems have worn away, and a sophisticated audience knowledge has taken their place, a pervasive realization that the media consist, like other manufacturing and bureaucratic activities, of a network of processes and procedures.

The grand project of verisimilitude is turning back upon itself. We see *through* the images more than we see *of* them. We have begun to sense that the living realities are shaped by the processes and conventions. We know that the advertising of politicians is different from the advertising of goods, but the kinds of belief and acceptance we have been trained to offer are themselves exposed as the results of aesthetic convention; the arrangement of these has been disclosed to us, like the cracking of a code. But the code is built into the sensorium, and so the better we know the medium, the better we see through it.

Remember the jury who were repeatedly made to watch the video of the beating of Rodney King, and who yet refused to convict the policemen; were they not an extreme example of a new scepticism, a dethronement of the moving image, a delegitimization of the image as evidence? Our late twentieth-century eyes are being retrained to scan pages of luxuriant advertising, the filmed profiles of political leaders, the videoed confessions of hostages supplied by kidnappers, hours of television talk shows conducted on light-suffused interview couches, newsreels showing the uncontrolled mass mourning of thousands of North Korean citizens for their deceased leader Kim Il Sung – and yet to believe nothing of what we see. The culmination of the cult of the image is not the *demystification* that the radicals of the 1960s envisaged as a form of liberation, but our complete distrust of it. We have followed the long recursive progress of the image from perspective to virtual reality, and have acquired the precious knowledge of its synthetic and iconic roles – and thus, how to protect ourselves against them. What we take away from a century of the moving image is an institutionalized dis-illusion.

A range of images that retains its authority is one which is least dependent upon a human actor. The surveillance camera provides an ever-increasing flow of images of everything we do. Unlike the images of television, it records the least 'eventful' happenings. But under its gaze we all look as if our actions are criminal, since every deed captured by a surveillance camera contains the subliminal anticipation of criminality. It provides an eternal identity parade in which all manner of people are forced, consciously or unconsciously, to take part. In a modern city there are already so many surveillance cameras that one could extract from them detailed accounts of whole episodes of people's lives. The surveillance image makes all our lives appear secret, just as it reveals the banality of that secret. Here is another device of fiction, an imaginative reversal of potential. When the surveillance image is transferred to television, in the course of a fiction, it becomes intensely exciting, yielding the sense of the *ipsissimum* of a behaviour.

The surveillance camera carries the aura of authenticity, greatly and paradoxically assisted by the poor quality of the images. They are not set up, nor properly lit for photography; they are unrehearsed. There is no surprise, but there are clear, though disconnected, narrative threads if we choose to notice them. Their presence is precisely intended to reduce narrative actions, to render human behaviour less interesting. They are pure vision, the seeing eye that offers no insight, starts out with no theory. A woman unloads her shopping, opens her car and drives away. A stream of people pass through the door, speak to the reception desk and move on. A man walks through a dark alley, notices a passing woman but passes on. In the banality of surveillance perhaps lies the ultimate destination of the great realist aspiration.

Virtual reality is at the opposite end of the spectrum of banality. It proclaims its enthrallingness. It suggests itself as a tool of the imagination, and its epistemological convincingness is its very device. The perfection of its particular project of realism is its fiction. It is ultra-fiction contrived through ultra-realism, and its implications are at present being explored in science fiction more vigorously than in documentary or by the observing sciences. Already a new Cyberpunk subculture is preparing the way for a new wave of moral panics, for specialists will assuredly detect a new range of emerging dysfunctions, disorders and disorientating states of mind. The novels of William Gibson[23] stare into the new dystopic abyss, but at the same time seem to encourage a breathless sense of Utopias to come. J. G. Ballard is quoted as saying: 'Virtual reality, if it comes on stream, will represent the greatest challenge to the human race since the invention of language. The fact that an illusion of reality can be electronically created has all sorts of consequences that one cannot anticipate … it will enable us to fulfil, without hurting each other or even ourselves, all our most extraordinary and deviant fantasies … When we watch a murder mystery, we won't be watching someone else commit a crime, but if we want to we'll be able to play the criminal or the victim. For the first time we will be able to play with our own psychopathology as a game.'

Virtual reality has already made its appearances in cinematic science fiction, but is naturally held back by the sheer problem of re-representing virtual reality in conventional two-dimensional cinema. Brett Leonard's *Lawnmower Man* appeared in 1992.[24] It has a Frankensteinian plot. Dr Angelo has resigned from his job experimenting with the commercial use of virtual reality to increase the intelligence of chimpanzees; and he has taken his knowledge home with him. At home he attempts, successfully, to improve the mental capacities of a simple-minded gardener called Jobe, who develops telepathic and kinetic powers and attempts to plug himself into a world-wide computer.

Dr Angelo prevents this by the use of explosives, but Jobe's body disintegrates while he is still wearing his virtual reality data-suit. He is now trapped in the electronic world, taking Dr Angelo with him, and in the ultimate explosion, involving an awesome display of special effects, every telephone in the world begins to ring. Jobe seeks escape from the hostility of a world where, as a simpleton, he had been harassed and bullied, and he finds the liberating salvation of virtual reality, the Cyberworld. Dr Angelo and Jobe are transformed into Cybergods in the new realm of Virtual Reality, where good and evil have lost their meaning. A whole genre based on the recapitulation of such themes is perfect raw material for fresh moral panics. The press must be waiting to exploit this as soon as the medium enters into the common allusion of readers.

Appropriately enough, it is Dr Timothy Leary, guru of the 1960s drug culture who so alarmed an earlier generation of parents, who has now become a guru of the new movement. The movement does indeed have something in common with the psychedelic culture of thirty years ago, but differs in its emphasis on creating new *cybernetic* states of mind where drugs play no part. For in cyberspace, the body has no role to play. Cyberspace simultaneously offers an escape from consumer culture, from the market economy and from the problems of daily life, while providing admission to a rational electronic world where the creative and meditative coexist in contact with sophisticated technology. Paradoxically, virtual reality is an out-of-body experience. There is a powerful streak of anti-materialist New Ageism in the virtual reality subculture, but entrance is by credit card. For a time the international archpriest of the cult was Jaron Lanier, in appearance and approach a kind of New Mexican John the Baptist, who promises his followers both the pleasures of hallucination and a future with enhanced psychic powers. But virtual reality is at its heart a project of reindustrialization, and Lanier has been profiled in the *Wall Street Journal*.

The virtual reality subculture is a suggestion, a market preparation for technologies that are not yet in fact available. To see the potential of this new set of technologies, one must look at the military techniques deployed during the Gulf War of 1991. There is an uncomfortable mismatch between the prophetic proclamations of the gurus and the likely commercial forms the medium will take. It will undoubtedly offer the full range of practicable interactive fascinations, and the present clustering of novelists around virtual reality suggests that in due course there will be a new range of narrative and imaginative materials. But Mr Lanier's declared medium of peacefulness exists for the present only in its own two-dimensional shadow, in such phenomena as Nintendo war-games; but it was in the equivalent, one hundred years ago, that one would have had to search for the first fruits of cinema.

When you attempt to contemplate the issues, cultural, psychological, moral, economic, involved in Cyberspace, you may feel the same helpless disorientation as when, for example, you read about the breakdown in international control of enriched plutonium. You sense a world of reason spinning helplessly out of control. We are evolving a medium of contrived irrationalism in which the culture of pure argument dating back to the Enlightenment dissolves into a complexity of interactive improvisations. All versions of all ideas and theories disappear into an intellectual data-soup, from which we can extract instant simulations, myriad quotations, countless drafts and rehearsals. The science-fiction and cult derivations are in a way the most reliable aspects of the promised transformation. They have their evident ontologies and counterparts in other stages of our culture. We can cope with fictional monsters, whatever form they take;

youth cults infuse something new into our civilization and fade away in less than a decade, as the commercially minded inventors move through the constantly augmenting repertoire of new gadgets.

We are entering a new era, one might say a new realm, of high-definition, interactive and mutually convergent technologies of communication. Some of these belong under the rubric of 'Superhighway', others are part of the project of virtual reality, a yearning that can trace its origins back to the Renaissance preoccupation with perspective. But all of them, especially when taken together, presage a cultural shift, an alteration in the means of culture and therefore in the definitions of culture. They also imply a shift in the operations of the sensorium, that is, in the machinery of our mental response to cultural experience.

In the 1990s we suffer from a serious loss of nerve about using certain major terms and concepts, ones that T. S. Eliot satisfactorily defined for a whole generation. I am thinking not only of 'culture', but of 'tradition', 'elite', 'talent'. Eliot was the last man of letters who felt free to beat the bounds of this range of terminology. And in more recent times, notices against trespassing have been put up by sociologists, with visas rarely granted – even to poets.

To Eliot, culture meant 'a whole way of life' and encompassed 'all the characteristic activities of a people'. His definition drew something from anthropology, and something from Coleridge's idea of 'cultivation'. And it implied a sense of the permanence of the industrial system and its universalizing values. In his *Notes Towards the Definition of Culture*, Eliot provided his own list of these 'characteristic activities', which today evoke the faded world of Tom Hopkinson's *Picture Post* England, a pre-Cold War, Laskiesque society of mutually (though grudgingly) accepted class differences: the Eliot list includes Derby Day but also Cowes and the Henley Regatta, the dog race, the pin-table, the dartboard, the music of Elgar, and 'cabbage cut into sections'. In our generation we have become more intensely concerned with the definition of culture, but in societies that have become subdivided into micro-cultures of generations and ethnicities, there seems little chance now of making common property out of all the available traded and approved lists of 'characteristic activities'. It will be interesting to see whether the new means of culture, with its promise to blur the lines between authentic and oneiric, universal and individual, real and imagined, will revive the possibility.

The Future of Entertainment –
a speculation [1]

During the twentieth century the whole concept of entertainment has altered from that of a group of activities interposed at the edges of the working day to that of a group of industries which see their role as providing for the totality of leisure time available in a society. Entertainment was, for the great majority, a communal experience, something mostly available outside the home, but at the end of the twentieth century we can see how entertainment has gradually taken over the home, and indeed has transformed its organization.

McKechnie's history of popular entertainments, published early this century, lists the following in its chapter headings: mimes, minstrels and strolling players, fun-fairs, Punch and Judy, pantomime, music-halls, the circus and the cinematograph. Theatre and opera would not have been considered popular forms, in Britain at any rate, nor would art galleries or tourism. Museums were education, not entertainment. Newspapers and magazines were not run by people who thought of themselves as part of the entertainment business – although they were beginning to. Public houses and restaurants were there to satisfy needs, rather than to consume the leisure time of working people.

It has been more than television that has brought about this transformation in the concept of entertainment. The greatest change has been that people can now expect to have their own homes, whether they live as families or as individuals. The advent of television in the 1950s was made possible not only by the availability of new spending power and by the demand for mass entertainment, but simply because of the spread of private family accommodation, owned or rented. The television receiver was a prime item of furniture in the vast numbers of homes built outside the Victorian and Edwardian cities of Europe and America. The Macmillan electoral victory of 1959, which played upon a tremendous sense of individual and family well-being, was the result of the kept promise to build more than 300,000 homes a year. Television programmes and advertising helped in the acquisition and furnishing of homes, which were the primary aesthetic concerns (as well as the primary economic decisions) of that generation.

You have first to imagine the future of the home and the family as a unit if you wish to make predictions about the future of entertainment. The family was inscribed deeply into the culture of the television medium in its opening decade, the 1950s. But by the late 1960s a new generation was struggling to get out of the home, and these discontents, reflected in the youth culture and the inter-generational tensions of the time, forced a change in the whole approach of radio as well as television. The audience was to some extent reconceptualized into groups and specialized interests. The arrival of the video recorder, and in America of cable television too, has contributed to this process of change; more programmes (and channels) emerged that were designed for sections of the audience. But television remains constrained by the 'family' expectations still held of it, even though by the 1990s there were children present only in 23 per cent of homes in Britain. During these long years of recession the home has also become the location of our frustrated economic expectations.

You can see the changes reflected in television soap opera. For British viewers, the vexations of *Brookside* and *Eastenders*, as well as the *Eldorado* people with their unadmired aspirations, have usurped the comfortable certainties of *Coronation Street*. One might predict, therefore, that in the coming decades a new generation will welcome entertainment that assists their escape from the home into places less fraught with social and financial stress. A new tendency towards the big, outdoor, electronics-assisted spectacle is under way. In the vast blockbuster movies of Spielberg, in the spread of Disneylands, and in the transformation of museums – but also in the spread of the mobile phone and in the emerging new medium of virtual reality – there are pointers towards the start of both a new solipsism and a mass exodus into the cultural outdoors.

Moreover, leisure time is growing at such a rate that the home can no longer remain its principal locus.

Because of the increase in life expectation, combined with gradually decreasing working hours and a later start to working life (not to speak of endemic unemployment), the proportion of the average lifetime devoted to work is diminishing. In 1981 there were 11.3 million people over the age of 60 in Britain; by the end of the century that figure will have risen by very little, to 12 million, but only half of them will still be at work. Twenty years beyond that, there will be 20 million inhabitants over 60, and a third of the whole population – now much healthier than in the past – will be over the age of 55. For a large section of them the retirement age will fall even further, and people will expect to live for 25 years after they cease work; at the start of the century people could expect to live for only five rather exhausted years after retiring.

Moreover, the working week will for most people last no

more than 35 hours, with ten weeks of holiday a year. But the most significant prediction, provided by the Henley Forecasting Centre, is that the average number of working *years* will fall to 35 (it was closer to 48 years earlier in the century). So the ages of man will consist of 20 years of childhood, education and the search for career or work, followed by 35 of work, and ending in 25 of retirement. What can one speculate about the mind-set of such a generation that might tell us something of its likely needs in entertainment?

Even by the year 2000, everyone over the age of 50 will have been born in the post-war era, and will share that era's expectations in terms of housing and education; the generation of people whose early lives, and whose parents' lives, engendered the low expectations of the 1930s will have gone. The sense of having been rescued from the bad old days that still tinges our attitudes in the 1990s will have evaporated. The media will have educated the public into a desire for ever-proliferating forms of satisfaction. Their beliefs will no doubt become greener, and they will have the time to be more socially and morally concerned. It is the coming dominance of the population by this group, already numerous, that prompts supermarkets to provide a selection of three dozen different brands of bottled water. One can expect this band of the population to become hostile to the use of personal transport, and to become highly conscious of the danger of spending leisure time in ozone-free sunshine. Their avidity for making choices will perhaps make the very processes of private selection and tailoring of information important characteristics of culture at all levels.

So there are two parallel trends, of opposite kinds, that may come to characterize the next era in entertainment: on the one hand, the big, spectacular, communal experience will return, with stylish venues and media aided by technology; this will become, as it were, the circus of the twenty-first century. The prevailing aesthetic will demand the most completely convincing representations, whether of history, contemporary events or fantasy. Movies, theme parks, operatic *tours de force*, will be labour-intensive, with large casts whether of actors or technicians. On the other hand, there will be the consequences of the virtually inevitable mass take-up of interactivity, which has long been predicted on the basis of the new IT devices already available. If you attempt to link these two tendencies – the public spectacle and the capacity for individual choice – you arrive at a medium of dial-up virtual reality: individuals or small groups using interactive techniques to gain access to an intangible but wholly enthralling experience, giving the solitary individual the feeling of being present at a spectacle in the illusory company of large numbers of others. You may be sure that somewhere in Japan someone is thinking hard about it, this combination of VOD (Video on Demand) and VR (Virtual Reality).

Interactivity in information media entails both the ability on the part of the receiver to choose the programme transmitted to him or her, but also the facility to manipulate multiple choices of direction within a programme. The viewer might be watching a sporting event, live or recorded, and decide to interrupt it to watch an interview with the team captain, or see the highlights of a previous game, or replay highlights from the current game, in real time or slow motion. The transmitting company might also be taking bets from viewers on the eventual winner and score of the live game. VOD services would depend on the availability of very large stockpiles of recorded films and programmes (and the negotiation and acquisition of retransmission rights in these by the vendor) and the computerization of all billing and handling. The gap between the physical practicability of such a system and its realization would be at least a generation, not least because it would depend upon a new level of mass disposable income and a very patient investor. The task is complicated physically, legally and financially.

For example, a pioneering Canadian cable company called Videotron runs a service that enables viewers to choose the angles of the shots in a football match and make the camera focus on particular players in an orchestra. Philips's new CD-1 machine provides an early impression of VOD by enabling you to choose 'interactively' from the material on a CD slotted into a domestic television receiver. The two provide a glimpse of what might come with the synergetic combination of a full-scale video library and a really versatile electronic selection system. Over the next twenty or thirty years commercial systems will certainly arrogate the terminology, although for the time being the rather optimistically supplied services are merely interim measures.

Such a development must depend on the establishment of much more plentiful telecommunications connections and switching facilities than currently exist. One of Clinton's 1992 election pledges was to revitalize the US economy by creating a 'data superhighway' comparable to the interstate highway system constructed in the 1950s. It might be more apt to think of it as a substitute for Reagan's 'Star Wars' project. As a senator, Al Gore campaigned enthusiastically for a decade for a data super-highway. Now the Clinton administration has submitted a $5 billion proposal to develop the necessary software system over four years, and private companies have started to volunteer to construct parts of the eventual vast transmission system. Neither telephone nor cable companies are yet ready to build a fully interactive data highway reaching from coast to coast, but there are hints of what might come in future years. For example, GTE has installed in a part of California a system that lets customers pay bills and play games down an ordinary multi-channel cable. The superhighway is several decades away, though, and such projects merely provide experience and some foundations for an interactive information and entertainment system.

At one time it was thought that the data highway would only be possible by using optic fibre in great quantity for all linkages, inter-city, local and domestic – an extraordinarily large-scale retooling which it was estimated some years ago would cost anything up to $500 billion dollars to set up in America alone. But it is now becoming possible to get much more data through existing telephone wires, including an adequate but not yet high-definition video signal. Scientists at Bellcore are optimistic of making further improvements that would reduce the cost of creating the means for pouring large quantities of data of all kinds duo-directionally and interactively. In more recent years, of course, fibre-optic techniques have been used in Internet, the network that has now become so extensive as to be almost the symbol of the decade.

The US government will not itself create the new network, even though that is the impression many people gained during the Clinton campaign. The administration does, however, intend to press ahead with many of the development costs, and to create the necessary legislation to end the legal divisions between cable and telephone providers that have prevented progress. The legal changes would encourage private industry to invest more heavily in the new techniques, uninhibited by old prohibitions that kept telephone out of television and cable out of telephony. The result could be, in the rather distant future, that the US would develop a national interactive data system which would enable all forms of data – from libraries, billing systems and general administration to many forms of entertainment – to be accessible to every home, interactively. The opportunity for every subscriber to make multiple choices and demands is the essence of the quest. It implies an electronic free market extended, on the grand scale, into the domestic sphere.

The rise of the CD in the last decade is the result of a search for the most complete form of illusion in sound. We want to feel that we are not listening to a recording, but enjoying direct contact with music at the source. The same desire is latent in respect of moving images. People will be induced to invest again in a new range of video equipment when it brings them a more intense and enthralling image. That is why great investments have been made for decades now in high-definition television, or HDTV. Japanese, American and European manufacturers, governments and technical standards-makers have been negotiating and politely squabbling over the geopolitics of HDTV ever since colour television reached saturation in Western television markets.

But the number of scanning lines is by no means the only issue involved in improving the quality of the television image so that it approaches the condition of virtual reality. The aspect ratio needs to become oblong, rather than almost square as it is now. The cathode-ray tube needs to be replaced by something flatter and more portable. The several existing forms of television (PAL, NTSC, SECAM) need to be made interchangeable across the geographic barriers that separate them today. It ought to be possible to translate the image from one frame-rate per second to another, and transcode it from one line-standard to another. The image needs to become completely interchangeable and interconnectable internationally, as well as visually sharper and of a different shape. In itself, HDTV represents really only one part of this change. Only complete digitization of all video and television would enable the world to move ahead from one state of video to another. A fully digitized signal could carry the additional information necessary to achieve all the decoding and recoding. A film or television signal could find its way into all standards of recording and all existing television systems. What is required is the creation of an 'intelligent' television alongside an HDTV system. That would circumvent the problems of HDTV as its various intending practitioners try to coax (or hoax) the world into accepting one technical standard or another.

HDTV will provide an important boost for everyone in the movie and television industries, as well as those involved in outdoor spectacle, advertising and theatrical entertainment. It will enable all images to become that much more convincing, to suggest themselves as being real, whether in two- or three-dimensional formats. Few people have yet experienced the newly touted medium of virtual reality, but excitement is necessarily less than complete in a medium where the subject is compelled to wear goggles. What one can envisage emerging in future decades is a virtual reality available in booths, perhaps sited in the shopping and entertainment areas of cities, and perhaps eventually turning into a home device. With the addition of interactivity, and with a library available, it could become a viable technology of entertainment, for in due course it is sure to attract writers and artists of talent.

This would be the apt culmination of the twentieth century's endless search for profuse and entrancing escapist devices – the end of a path that leads from the Walkman, which first began to demonstrate to the technological visionaries of the entertainment industry that people are ready for a new generation of addictive and imaginatively captivating devices. The individual of tomorrow would be subject to greater isolation, though of a self-pleasuring kind, and the lonely Disneylands of the future are at least a stimulating substitute for lonely idleness. But they could do much for traditional media such as museums, which could exploit the potential of exact similitude in wonderful ways: one could walk into the gallery of the Elgin Marbles and be transported back to ancient Greece. One could go into one's local museum and be offered a trip to the streets and squares as they were in former times. These might be rather more effective than the heavy, rented, sound-only devices currently on offer at art shows and exhibitions.

Of course, all these developments are aspects of, and subject to, the wider transformations being wrought by IT in the worlds of information, science, commerce, industry, defence. But entertainment is crucial to the forms they will take and the uses to which they will be put. Entertainment reflects something of the psychic drives that lie deeper than the immediate demands of the market. It is not possible, as a British minister in the 1980s hoped, for an 'entertainment-led' IT revolution to occur. But the entertainment industry, alongside the health industry, is as close as any other to the things that people actually want and are willing to pay for. In the next generation they will want far more diversion, as the spending of time becomes the central problem (or opportunity) of life. Ingenuity in offering new forms of entertainment is likely to provide much of the drive for the big technological leaps.

NOTES

PREFACE

1. Gissing, George, *New Grub Street* (1891), London, 1958, p. 5.
2. Eco, Umberto, *Apocalypse Postponed*, London, 1994, p. 18.
3. Williams, Raymond, *Culture and Society*, London, 1958, p. 195.
4. *Ibid.*, p. 321.
5. London, 1948.

I

1. Auden, W. H., *Secondary Words*, London, 1968.
2. Heaney, Seamus, *The Governments of the Tongue*, London, 1988, pp. 91–108.
3. Johnson, Samuel, *The History of Rasselas, Prince of Abyssinia* (1759).
4. 'Poets are ... the trumpets which sing to battle, and feel not what they inspire; the influence which is moved not, but moves. Poets are the unacknowledged legislators of the world.' Shelley, P. B., 'A Defence of Poetry' (1821), in *Shelley's Literary Criticism*, ed. John Shawcross, London, 1932, p. 159.
5. Wilde, Oscar, 'The Decay of Lying' in *Essays*, ed. Pearson, London, 1950, p. 232.
6. See Goldie, Mark, 'J. N. Figgis and the History of Political Thought in Cambridge' in *Cambridge Minds*, ed. Richard Mason, Cambridge, 1994, pp. 177–92. Also Figgis, John Neville, *The Divine Right of Kings* (1914).
7. In *Tradition and the Individual Talent*, 1919.

II

1. See Kristeller, Paul Oskar, *Renaissance Thought and the Arts*, Princeton, NJ, 1990, especially Chapter IX, 'The Modern System of the Arts'.

2. The ancients' separation of gentlemanly activities from the reverse had been reconfirmed for the medieval mind by Aquinas who, in a commentary on Aristotle, makes the distinction between the good things which are 'praiseworthy' (i.e. those which are useful for an end) and those which are 'honourable' (i.e. those which are useful in themselves).

3. See the conclusion to Eisenstein, Elizabeth, *The Printing Press as Agent of Change*, Cambridge, 1979.

4. See Condivi, Ascanio, *Life of Michelangelo Buonarroti* (1553), trans. George Bull, Oxford, 1992: 'Michelangelo gave up dissecting corpses. This was because his long familiarity with the practice had so upset his stomach that he could neither eat nor drink beneficially' (p. 63).

5. See Ghyka, Matila, *The Geometry of Art and Life*, New York, 1977.

6. Alberti, Leon Battista, *On Painting*, trans. Cecil Grayson, London, 1972, p. 72. With thanks to Deanna M. McHugh's 'The Influence of Art and Science – Figural Proportions and Anatomy in the Florentine Renaissance', unpublished thesis, University of California, 1993.

7. Vasari, Giorgio, *Lives of the Artists* (1550), trans. George Bull, London, 1987.

8. Kristeller, *ibid.*, pp. 177–8.

9. *Encyclopédie*, vol. 1, 1752. See also his essay entitled 'Beau' in volume 2.

10. *Spectator*, No. 411. Addison alludes to the pleasures that proceed from nature and to those secondary pleasures that proceed from the arts which imitate nature.

11. Akenside, Mark, *The Pleasures of Imagination* (1744, new edition 1757), echoes Addison: '… all the various entertainments we meet with, either in poetry, painting, music, or any of the elegant arts.'

12. Coleridge, Samuel Taylor, *Biographia Literaria*, London, 1906, pp. 85–92.

13. Coleridge, Samuel Taylor, *On the Constitution of Church and State*, 1837, section 5.

14. *The Friend*, section 2, essay 11, 1818. Quoted by Raymond Williams in *Culture and Society 1780–1950*, London, 1958, pp. 68–9.

15. *Biographia Literaria*, pp. 145–6.

16. Sidney, Philip, *An Apology for Poetry*, ed. Geoffrey Shepherd, Edinburgh, 1965. See also Lipking, Lawrence, *The Ordering of the Arts in 18th-Century England*, Princeton, NJ, 1970.

17. Kristeller, *op. cit.*, p. 221.

18. See Frayling, Christopher, *The Royal College of Art: 150 Years of Arts and Design*, London, 1987.

19. Quoted *ibid.*, p. 8.

20. Brooke, Rupert, *Democracy and the Arts*, London, 1946, p. 13.

III

1. Habermas, Jürgen, *The Structural Transformation of the Public Sphere: An Inquiry into a Category of Bourgeois Society*, trans. Thomas Burger and Frederick Lawrence, Cambridge, 1989.

2. For example, in Foucault, Michel, *The Order of Things: An Archaeology of the Human Sciences*, London, 1970, and the same author's *Madness and Civilisation: A History of Insanity in the Age of Reason*, London, 1971.

3. Reynolds, Sir Joshua, *Discourses on Art*, ed. Robert R. Wark, New Haven, Conn., 1975.

4. Barrell, John, *The Political Theory of Painting from Reynolds to Hazlitt; 'The Body of the Public'*, New Haven, Conn., 1986.

5. Public Law 632, 69th Congress, Feb 23, 1927. The phrase 'public interest, convenience, necessity' was taken by President Coolidge from American public utility legislation and used as the discretionary licensing standard. The wording was then retained in the Communications Act of 1934 (Public Law 416, 73rd Congress, June 19, 1934). This, with various amendments, has remained the basis of US broadcasting law.

6. Arnold, Matthew, *Culture and Anarchy* (1869), ed. with intro by J. Dover Wilson, Cambridge, 1969, pp. 70–1.

7. *Ibid.*, p. 70.

8. Newman, J. H., *On the Scope and Nature of University Education*, lectures delivered in Dublin in 1852. *Lectures on Universities* appeared in 1859, and *The Idea of a University*, containing both texts, in 1873. Newman held that a university's prime duty was teaching, not research, to train the mind rather than to disseminate knowledge.

9. Arnold, *op. cit.*, pp. 72–97.

10. In *Culture and Society*, London, 1958, p. 126.

11. Reith, J. C. W., *Broadcast Over Britain*, London, 1925.

12. Report of the Committee on the Future of Broadcasting (Chairman: Lord Annan), London, 1977, p. 14, para 2.26. 'The ideals of middle-class culture, so felicitously expressed by Matthew Arnold a century ago, which had created a continuum of taste and opinion, always susceptible to change and able to absorb the avant-garde within its own urbane, liberal, flexible principles, found it ever more difficult to accommodate the new expressions of life in the sixties. The new vision of life reflected divisions within society ...'

13. Told in Barnouw, Erik, *A Tower in Babel: A History of Broadcasting in the United States*, New York, 1966, pp. 247–8.

14. Lippmann, Walter, *Public Opinion*, New York, 1922 (rev. 1929).

15. Angell, Norman, *The Public Mind: Its Disorders, its Exploitation*, London, 1926, and *The Press and the Organisation of Society*, London, 1923.

16. Barnouw, *op. cit.*, quoting from *Radio Broadcast* 1922

17. Hoover, Herbert, *Memoirs of Herbert Hoover: The Cabinet and the Presidency 1920-33*, New York, 1952, pp. 139–40.

18. See Barnouw, *op. cit.*, p. 96.

19. See the account of the growth of the popular press in Williams, Raymond, *The Long Revolution*, London, 1961, pp. 197–8.

20. Fowler, Mark, and Brenner, D. L., 'A Market-place Approach to Broadcast Regulation', reprinted in *Mass Communication Review Yearbook*, ed. Wartella, Ellen, Whitney, D. C., and Windahl, S., Beverly Hills, Calif., 1983, vol. 4, pp. 645–95.

21. The main body of doctrine relating to fairness expected to be observed by American broadcasters was enshrined in the Section 315 Primer (*Use of Broadcast Facilities by Candidates for Public Office*, 31 Fed. Reg. 6660, adopted April 27, 1966) in which the Federal Communications Commission set out to interpret its own rules, as well as Section 315 of the Communications Act of 1934.

22. Report of the Committee on Financing the BBC (Chairman: Professor Alan Peacock DSC FBA), London, 1986.

23. See, for example, Habermas, Jürgen, *The Theory of Communicative Action*, Boston, 1984, vol. 1.

24. Dewey, John, *The Public and its Problems*, New York, 1927.

25. *The Future of the BBC: Serving the Nation, Competing World-wide*, London, 1994. This was the Department of National Heritage's response to the BBC's own document *Extending Choice: The BBC's Role in the New Broadcasting Age*, London, 1992.

26. *The Public Service Idea in British Broadcasting: Main Principles*, London, 1985, 1988.

27. See Bourdieu, Pierre, *Distinction: A Social Critique of the Judgement of Taste*, Harvard, 1984.

28. Carey, James, *Communication as Culture: Essays on Media and Society*, Boston, 1989, p. 19.

29. *Ibid.*, p. 34.

30. Berlin, Isaiah, *Two Concepts of Liberty; His Inaugural Lecture of October 1958*, Oxford, p. 52.

31. Eliot, T. S., *Ash Wednesday*.

32. Boyle, Andrew, *Only the Wind Will Listen: Reith of the BBC*, London, 1972.

IV

1. Eliot, T. S., *Notes Towards the Definition of Culture*, London, 1948, Chapter One: The Three Senses of Culture.

2. Geertz, Clifford, *The Interpretation of Cultures*, 1973, 1993.

3. Quoted by Geertz, *op. cit.*, p. 47, from Tylor, E. B., *Primitive Culture*.

4. See Waldrop, Mitchell, *Complexity: The Emerging Science at the Edge of Order and Chaos*, London, 1994.

5. See Kuhn, Thomas S., *The Structure of Scientific Revolutions*, Chicago, 2nd ed. 1970.

6. The *Novum Organum* ('New Instrument') was published in 1620. Its intention was to describe, through a number of aphorisms, the method by which knowledge was to be universalized.

7. See Smith, John Maynard, 'Life at the Edge of Chaos', *New York Review of Books*, vol. 42, No. 4, March 1995.

8. Bell, Daniel, *The Coming of Post-Industrial Society: A Venture in Social Forecasting*, London, 1974; and see Bell's chapter 'The Social Framework of the Information Society' in *Microelectronics Revolution*, ed. Tom Forester, Oxford, 1980; Machlup, Fritz, *The Production and Distribution of Knowledge in the USA*, Princeton, NJ, 1980.

9. See the Prologue to Mathias, Peter, *The First Industrial Nation: An Economic History of Britain 1700–1914*, Methuen, 1983, pp. 1–23.

10. Machlup's book was greatly influenced by the statistics compiled several years earlier by Marc Porat and published as *The Information Economy: Definition and Measurement*, Washington DC, 1977.

11. Al Gore, speech given at the Superhighway Summit, 11 January 1994, Academy of Arts and Sciences, Los Angeles.

12. *Ibid.* and see McQuaille, Tom, 'The USA's Information Infrastructure Falls to the Republicans and the Corporate Players' in *Intermedia*, December/January 1994-5, vol. 22, No. 4.

13. Nora, Simon, and Minc, Alain, *The Computerisation of Society*, Cambridge, Mass., 1980.

14. Masuda, Yonedji, *The Information Society as Postindustrial Society*, Bethesda, Md., 1981.

15. Tama New Town, near Tokyo.

16. Ellul, Jacques, *The Technological Society*, trans. John Wilkinson, New York, 1964.

17. Roszak, Theodore, *The Cult of Information*, New York, 1986.

18. Shallis, Michael, *The Silicon Idol*, Oxford, 1984; Reinecke, Ian, *Electronic Illusions*, London, 1984; Wicklein, John, *Electronic Nightmare: The Home Communications Set and Your Freedom*, Boston, Mass., 1981.

19. Beniger, James R., *The Control Revolution: Technological and economic Origins of the Information Society*, Cambridge, Mass., 1986.

20. See Wardrop, Mitchell, *op. cit.*, for discussion of the concept of 'emergent states'.

V

1. See the Introduction to Jameson, Fredric, *Postmodernism, or The Cultural Logic of the Late Capitalism*, London, 1991.

2. Baudelaire, Charles, 'The Salon of 1859', *Art in Paris 1845-62*, London, 1965, p.153, quoted by Noël Burch in an article entitled 'Charles Baudelaire versus Frankenstein' in *Afterimage* 8/9, Spring 1981, pp. 4-23, reprinted in *Modern Art and Modernism: A Critical Anthology*, ed. Francis Fresana and Charles Harrison, London, 1982, pp. 19-27.

3. 'The photograph ... carries with it more than mere resemblance, namely a kind of identity'. Bazin, André, *What is Cinema?*, Berkeley, Calif., 1967, vol. 1, p. 96.

4. *Kino-Eye: The Writings of Dziga Vertov*, ed. Annette Michelson, trans. K. O'Brien, Berkeley, Calif., 1984.

5. Lowe, Donald M., *The History of Bourgeois Perception*, Brighton, 1982, p. 5.

6. Sontag, Susan, *On Photography*, London, 1978, 'To collect photographs is to collect the world', p. 3.

7. See David Ayerst's discussion of the coming of Pitman in *The Guardian: Biography of a Newspaper*, London, 1971.

8. Moberly Bell, C. F. See *The History of* The Times, vol. 3, 1884–1912.

9. See Virilio, Paul, *The Vision Machine*, London, 1994, pp. 1-19.

10. See the account of Donatello's techniques and discoveries in Vasari, Giorgio, *Lives of the Artists*, trans. George Bull, London, 1987, vol. 1, pp. 174-90.

11. See article by Wollen, Tana, 'The Bigger the Better, From Cinemascope to Imax' in *Future Visions: New Technologies of the Screen*, ed. Philip Hayward and Tana Wollen, London, 1993, pp. 10-30.

12. Auerbach, Erich, *Mimesis: The Representation of Reality in Western Literature*, trans. Willard R. Track, Princeton, NJ, 1974.

13. Benjamin, Walter, *Reflections*, ed. Peter Demetz, New York, 1978.

14. See Ceram, C. W., *Archaeology of the Cinema*, London, 1965; Sadoul, Georges, *Histoire générale du cinéma* (5 vols), Paris, 1946-54.

15. Marey, E. J., *Movement*, London, 1895; *Animal Mechanism: A Treatise on Terrestrial and Aerial Locomotion*, London, 1874.

16. A New Zealand artist of the 1930s who was a friend of Humphrey Jennings, the British documentarist. See Bendazzi, Giuseppe, *Cartoons*, London, 1994. Also a film by Keith Griffiths entitled *Doodlin'* , 1988.

17. I am indebted to Ian Christie for much of this information. See also Sadoul, *op. cit.*

18. See the article by Binkley, Timothy, 'Refiguring Culture', in Hayward and Wollen, *op. cit.*, pp. 92-122.

19. See Chapter 18, 'Patterns and Analogies', in Gilder, George, *Microcosm: The Quantum Revolution in Economics and Technology*, New York, 1989, pp. 235-6.

20. For a good account of this controversy, see Searle, John R., Churchland, Paul M., and Churchland, Patricia Smith, 'Artificial Intelligence: A debate', *Scientific American*, January 1990, vol. 26, 2:1.

21. See Mitchell, William, *City of Bits*, London, 1995.

22. See Romanyshyn, Robert, *Technology as Symptom and Dream*, London, 1989.

23. Gibson, William: *Neuromancer*, London, 1986 and 1994; *Virtual Light*, London, 1993 and 1994.

24. See review by Mark Kermode, *Sight and Sound*, June 92, vol 2:2, p. 43.

1. Published originally in 'The Future Surveyed', special supplement of *The Economist*, 11 September 1993, pp. 82-7.